Troubleshooting vSphere Storage

Become a master at troubleshooting and solving
common storage issues in your vSphere environment

Mike Preston

BIRMINGHAM - MUMBAI

Troubleshooting vSphere Storage

First published: November 2013

Production Reference: 1131113

Published by Packt Publishing Ltd.
Livery Place
35 Livery Street
Birmingham B3 2PB, UK.

ISBN 978-1-78217-206-2

www.packtpub.com

Cover Image by Aniket Sawant (aniket_sawant_photography@hotmail.com)

Credits

Author
Mike Preston

Reviewers
Jason Langer
Mario Russo
Aravind Sivaraman
Eric Wright

Acquisition Editor
Owen Roberts

Commissioning Editor
Shaon Basu

Technical Editors
Kanhucharan Panda
Vivek Pillai

Project Coordinator
Aboli Ambardekar

Proofreader
Jenny Blake

Indexer
Mariammal Chettiyar

Graphics
Yuvraj Mannari

Production Coordinator
Arvindkumar Gupta

Cover Work
Arvindkumar Gupta

About the Author

Mike Preston is an IT professional and an overall tech enthusiast living in Ontario, Canada. He has held all sorts of IT titles over the last 15 years including Network Technician, Systems Administrator, Programmer Analyst, Web Developer, and Systems Engineer in all sorts of different verticals, from sales to consulting. Currently, he is working as a Systems Analyst supporting the education market near his home in Belleville, Ontario.

Mike has always had an intense passion for sharing his skills, solutions, and work with various online communities, most recently focusing on the virtualization communities. He is an avid blogger at `blog.mwpreston.net` and participates in many discussions on Twitter (`@mwpreston`). It's his passion for sharing within the virtualization community which has led to Mike receiving the vExpert award for 2012 and 2013.

Mike has presented at VMworld, VMUGs, and various virtualization conferences on numerous times both as a customer and an overall evangelist and has published different whitepapers and articles for various tech websites. His commitment to giving back to the community has resulted in his most recent venture of becoming a Toronto VMUG co-leader. He is a VMware Certified Professional in Datacenter Virtualization on both Version 4 and 5 of vSphere and is currently pursuing his VCAP5-DCA, which he hopes to accomplish by 2014.

Acknowledgment

Firstly, I would like to thank my wife Alicia for putting up with all my late night and early morning writing sessions. I would also like to thank my two children, Hayden and Clara. Without their support, the completion of this book would have been nearly impossible.

Secondly, I would like to thank my technical reviewers Jason Langer, Eric Wright, and Angelo Luciani. Having those powerful brains comb over my work is one of the best decisions I ever made.

Lastly, I would like to thank the virtualization community. Without the many hours donated by the mentors, vRockstars, and others involved in the community, I would certainly not have been able to accomplish a project of this size. It's definitely a welcoming and helpful community and I'm humbled and happy to be a part of it.

About the Reviewers

Jason Langer works as a Solutions Architect for a VMware partner in the Pacific Northwest region helping customers achieve their datacenter virtualization goals. Jason has obtained multiple levels of certification both from Microsoft and VMware and brings 15 years of IT experience to the table. When not working his day job, Jason is active in the VMware community as a member of the Seattle VMUG Steering Committee and generating content for his blog, `virtuallanger.com`.

He is also currently working as a technical reviewer for *VMware ESXi 5.1 Cookbook*, *Mohammed Raffic Kajamoideen, Packt Publishing*.

Mario Russo has worked as an IT Architect, a Senior Technical VMware Trainer, and in the pre-sales department. He has also worked on VMware technology since 2004.

In 2005, he worked for IBM on the First Large Project Consolidation for Telecom Italia on the Virtual VMware ESX 2.5.1 platform in Italy with **Physical to Virtual (P2V)** tool.

In 2007, he conducted a drafting course and training for BancoPosta, Italy, and project disaster and recovery (DR Open) for IBM and EMC.

In 2008, he worked for the Project Speed Up Consolidation BNP and the migration P2V on VI3 infrastructure at BNP Cardif Insurance.

He is a **VMware Certified Instructor** (**VCI**) and is certified in VCAP5-DCA.

He is also the owner of Business to Virtual, which specializes in virtualization solutions.

He was also the technical reviewer of the book, *Implementing VMware Horizon View 5.2, Jason Ventresco, Packt Publishing*.

> I would like to thank my wife Lina and my daughter Gaia. They're my strength.

Aravind Sivaraman is a Virtualization Engineer with more than seven years of experience in the IT industry and for the past five years, he has been focused on virtualization solutions especially on VMware products. He has been awarded with the VMware vExpert title for the year 2013. He is a **VMware Technology Network (VMTN)** contributor and maintains his personal blog at `http://aravindsivaraman.wordpress.com/`. He can also be followed on Twitter (`@ss_aravind`).

I would like to thank my wife and my family members for supporting me towards the contribution of this book.

Eric Wright is a Systems Architect and VMware vExpert with a background in virtualization, business continuity, PowerShell scripting, and systems automation in many industries including financial services, health services, and engineering firms. As the author behind `www.DiscoPosse.com`, a technology and virtualization blog, Eric is also a regular contributor to community driven technology groups such as the VMUG organization in Toronto, Canada. You can connect with Eric at `www.twitter.com/DiscoPosse`.

When Eric is not working in technology, you may find him with a guitar in his hand or riding a local bike race or climbing over the obstacles on a Tough Mudder course. Eric also commits time regularly to charity bike rides and running events to help raise awareness and funding for cancer research through a number of organizations.

I wish I could thank everyone personally, but let me say thank you to my family, friends, and the very special people who've inspired me to be involved with technology. Thank you to the amazing and very accepting technology community who have helped me to be able to share my knowledge and to learn from the amazing minds that drive this incredible community.

www.PacktPub.com

Support files, eBooks, discount offers and more

You might want to visit www.PacktPub.com for support files and downloads related to your book.

Did you know that Packt offers eBook versions of every book published, with PDF and ePub files available? You can upgrade to the eBook version at www.PacktPub.com and as a print book customer, you are entitled to a discount on the eBook copy. Get in touch with us at service@packtpub.com for more details.

At www.PacktPub.com, you can also read a collection of free technical articles, sign up for a range of free newsletters and receive exclusive discounts and offers on Packt books and eBooks.

http://PacktLib.PacktPub.com

Do you need instant solutions to your IT questions? PacktLib is Packt's online digital book library. Here, you can access, read and search across Packt's entire library of books.

Why Subscribe?

- Fully searchable across every book published by Packt
- Copy and paste, print and bookmark content
- On demand and accessible via web browser

Free Access for Packt account holders

If you have an account with Packt at www.PacktPub.com, you can use this to access PacktLib today and view nine entirely free books. Simply use your login credentials for immediate access.

Instant Updates on New Packt Books

Get notified! Find out when new books are published by following @PacktEnterprise on Twitter, or the *Packt Enterprise* Facebook page.

Table of Contents

Preface

In 1998, a small company consisting of only five employees came out of stealth in Palo Alto, claiming to have successfully run Windows 95 on a virtual machine. This company was called VMware. Shortly thereafter, the first VMware product, a type 2 hypervisor dubbed Workstation 1.0 was released. In 2006, VMware really started to infiltrate the enterprise market with the release of ESX 3.0 and vCenter 2.0. Since then, the type 1 hypervisor ESX, now only ESXi, has been a major driver in providing business agility in bringing services to their customers.

When we think about many of the features that have been integrated into vSphere over the years, such as HA, vMotion, and Distributed Resource Scheduling; they all have shared one thing in common, storage requirements. With storage, more so shared storage becoming the core requirement behind many vSphere features, we need to ensure that when things go wrong, we have the tools and knowledge to identify issues, find root causes, and resolve problems as quickly as possible. When we look at the vSphere components, storage is most commonly the only item that is not local to the host. This means that with computer, memory, and network; the hosts provide the VMs with these local resources. Storage, for the most part, is a separate physical component and is shared amongst all of the hosts within your cluster, making it one of the most constrained resources and very difficult to troubleshoot.

Troubleshooting vSphere Storage provides a thorough overview of the concepts, steps, and information that vSphere administrators need to know in order to troubleshoot some of the most common storage related problems that spring up in a virtualized environment. This book provides you with the tools and knowledge that you need in order to discover and resolve the root cause of storage visibility, contention, performance, and capacity issues inside your vSphere environment.

What this book covers

In *Chapter 1, Understanding vSphere Storage Concepts and Methodologies*, we will get the base-level knowledge that we need in order to understand how storage inside a virtual environment functions. We will then learn the many ways in which vSphere identifies LUNs and datastores, key in any troubleshooting exercise involving storage.

In *Chapter 2, Commonly Used Tools for Troubleshooting Storage*, we will learn how to use the many different tools included within ESXi and vCenter that are referenced throughout the book. The fundamental knowledge of how to operate tools like esxtop is key to identifying the many storage related symptoms explained throughout the remaining chapters.

In *Chapter 3, Troubleshooting Storage Visibility*, we will delve into some of the most common steps we can take when our hosts are having issues connecting or seeing our storage. This chapter will cover the three major file transports; Fibre Channel, iSCSI, and NFS.

In *Chapter 4, Troubleshooting Storage Contention*, we will learn how to diagnose and troubleshoot one of the most common complaints by end users; slowness. By slowness, we mean storage performance and contention. We will look at the various symptoms of a performance problem, how to pinpoint the root causes, and finally some of the techniques and tools we can use to resolve them.

In *Chapter 5, Troubleshooting Storage Capacity and Overcommitment*, we will look at the risks that we take when implementing some of the biggest storage benefits that vSphere delivers. We will look how to effectively monitor our thinly-provisioned disks and arrays, how to protect and ensure that we aren't caught with rogue snapshots, and again, the various tools and techniques we can take to prevent issues from occurring.

In *Appendix A, Troubleshooting Steps*, we will highlight all of the various steps to take when certain issues appear, ensuring we are always taking a common approach when troubleshooting vSphere Storage.

In *Appendix B, Statistics of esxtop*, we will cover how to efficiently and interactively control the output from esxtop, and how to filter results, sort columns, and expand fields. We will also cover all of the most common storage statistics that are collected by esxtop, explaining what they represent, and at what threshold we should begin to investigate further.

In *Appendix C, iSCSI Error Codes*, we will learn how to decipher and understand the various error codes that the software iSCSI initiator will dump to our ESXi logfiles.

What you need for this book

In order to follow along with some of the troubleshooting exercises throughout this book, you will need at least one ESXi host, preferably managed by vCenter Server. Also, some of the counters, examples, and statistics mentioned throughout the book are only available if you are running vSphere 5.x or later.

Although the book is divided into chapters numbered sequentially, it is not a requirement that you follow them in order. *Chapter 1, Understanding vSphere Storage Concepts and Methodologies*, and *Chapter 2, Commonly Used Tools for Troubleshooting Storage*, will certainly give you an advantage when referencing the later chapters; however, how you chose to consume the information is completely up to you. My recommendation would be that once you have a solid understanding of the terminologies and tools listed in the first two chapters, that you chose the appropriate chapter afterwards depending on the type of issue you are troubleshooting; whether it be visibility (*Chapter 3, Troubleshooting Storage Visibility*), contention and performance (*Chapter 4, Troubleshooting Storage Contention*), or capacity and overcommitment (*Chapter 5, Troubleshooting Storage Capacity and Overcommitment*).

Who this book is for

This book is mainly geared towards vSphere administrators. Anyone who has responsibility for or looks after a VMware environment appreciates the fact that apart from managing the virtual infrastructure, they must have some knowledge of the components that attach to it; storage being one of the most important. This book will help the VMware administrators understand how to detect storage issues and resolve them by providing the "need to know" information about the various storage transports that ESXi utilizes.

Conventions

In this book, you will find a number of styles of text that distinguish between different kinds of information. Here are some examples of these styles, and an explanation of their meaning.

Code words in text are shown as follows: "In order to view a list of the PSA plugins, we use the `storage core` namespace of the `esxcli` command."

Any command-line input or output is written as follows:

```
esxcfg-scsidevs -c
```

New terms and **important words** are shown in bold. Words that you see on the screen, in menus or dialog boxes for example, appear in the text like this: "Select **Disk** under the **Resources** tab."

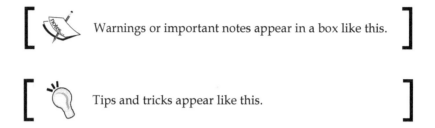

Warnings or important notes appear in a box like this.

Tips and tricks appear like this.

Reader feedback

Feedback from our readers is always welcome. Let us know what you think about this book—what you liked or may have disliked. Reader feedback is important for us to develop titles that you really get the most out of.

To send us general feedback, simply send an e-mail to feedback@packtpub.com, and mention the book title via the subject of your message.

If there is a topic that you have expertise in and you are interested in either writing or contributing to a book, see our author guide on www.packtpub.com/authors.

Customer support

Now that you are the proud owner of a Packt book, we have a number of things to help you to get the most from your purchase.

Errata

Although we have taken every care to ensure the accuracy of our content, mistakes do happen. If you find a mistake in one of our books—maybe a mistake in the text or the code—we would be grateful if you would report this to us. By doing so, you can save other readers from frustration and help us improve subsequent versions of this book. If you find any errata, please report them by visiting http://www.packtpub.com/submit-errata, selecting your book, clicking on the **errata submission form** link, and entering the details of your errata. Once your errata are verified, your submission will be accepted and the errata will be uploaded on our website, or added to any list of existing errata, under the Errata section of that title. Any existing errata can be viewed by selecting your title from http://www.packtpub.com/support.

Piracy

Piracy of copyright material on the Internet is an ongoing problem across all media. At Packt, we take the protection of our copyright and licenses very seriously. If you come across any illegal copies of our works, in any form, on the Internet, please provide us with the location address or website name immediately so that we can pursue a remedy.

Please contact us at `copyright@packtpub.com` with a link to the suspected pirated material.

We appreciate your help in protecting our authors, and our ability to bring you valuable content.

Questions

You can contact us at `questions@packtpub.com` if you are having a problem with any aspect of the book, and we will do our best to address it.

1
Understanding vSphere Storage Concepts and Methodologies

Before jumping into the details of how to troubleshoot vSphere Storage, it's best to understand the basics of how storage operates in a virtualized environment. On the whole, ESXi is a very user-friendly, easy-to-use hypervisor. However, when we look at it in terms of troubleshooting and storage, there are a lot of complex scenarios and key pieces of information that we need to know in order to resolve issues as they occur.

This chapter will help us to better understand the fundamentals of how vSphere and ESXi attach to and utilize various types of storage and show us how we can identify our datastores, storage paths, and LUNs within our environment. We will also learn about the **Pluggable Storage Architecture** (**PSA**) and take a broader look at how an application running in a virtual machine accesses storage.

The topics that we'll be covering in this chapter are:

- Storage virtualization
- Supported filesystems
- Storage naming
- The vSphere Pluggable Storage Architecture
- An I/O request—from start to finish

Storage virtualization

ESXi presents its storage to a VM using host-level storage virtualization techniques which essentially provide an abstraction layer between the actual physical storage, whether that is attached via a **Storage Area Network** (**SAN**), an Ethernet network or locally installed, and the virtual machines consuming the storage. This abstraction layer consists of many different components all working together to simulate that of a physical disk inside a virtual machine.

When a virtual machine is created, it will normally have at least one virtual disk assigned to it. When a virtual disk is assigned to a VM, a piece of virtual hardware called a virtual storage adapter is created in order to facilitate the communication between the VM and its underlying virtual hard disk (vmdk). The type of virtual storage adapter that is used greatly depends on the **Guest Operating System** setting that has been chosen for that specific VM (see the following table). This newly created SCSI adapter provides the interface between the OS and the VMkernel module on the ESXi host. The VMkernel module then locates the target file within the volume, maps the blocks from the virtual disk to the physical device, forwards the request through the Pluggable Storage Architecture, and finally queues the appropriate adapter on the ESXi host depending on the type of storage present (iSCSI NIC/Hardware Initiator, **Fibre Channel Host Bus Adapters** (**FC HBA**), NFS – NIC, or **Fibre Channel over Ethernet** (**FCoE** NIC/CNA)).

The following table outlines the various virtual SCSI adapters available:

Virtual SCSI adapter	Supported VM hardware version	Description	OS support
BusLogic Parallel	4,7,8,9,10	Emulates the BusLogic Parallel SCSI adapter. Mainly available for older operating systems.	Default for most Linux operating systems.
LSI Logic Parallel	4,7,8,9,10	Emulates the LSI Logic Parallel SCSI adapter. Supported by most new operating systems.	Default for Windows 2003/2003 R2.
LSI Logic SAS	7,8,9,10	Emulates the LSI Logic SAS adapter. Supported on most new operating systems.	Default for Windows 2008/2008 R2/2012.

Virtual SCSI adapter	Supported VM hardware version	Description	OS support
VMware Paravirtual SCSI (PVSCSI)	7,8,9,10	Purposely built to provide high throughput with a lower CPU overhead. Supported on select newer operating systems.	No defaults, but is supported with Windows 2003+, SUSE 11+, Ubuntu 10.04+, and RHEL6+.

Supported filesystems

VMware ESXi supports a couple of different filesystems to use as virtual machine storage; **Virtual Machine File System (VMFS)** and **Network File System (NFS)**.

VMFS

One of the most common ESXi storage configurations utilizes a purpose-built, high-performance clustered filesystem called VMFS. VMFS is a distributed storage architecture that facilitates concurrent read and write access from multiple ESXi hosts. Any supported SCSI-based block device, whether it is local, Fibre Channel, or network attached may be formatted as a VMFS datastore. See the following table for more information on the various vSphere supported storage protocols.

NFS

NFS, like VMFS, is also a distributed file system and has been around for nearly 20 years. NFS, however, is strictly network attached and utilizes **Remote Procedure Call (RPC)** in order to access remote files just as if they were stored locally. vSphere, as it stands today supports NFSv3 over TCP/IP, allowing the ESXi host to mount the NFS volume and use it for any storage needs, including storage for virtual machines. NFS does not contain a VMFS partition. When utilizing NFS, the NAS storage array handles the underlying filesystem assignment and shares in which ESXi simply attaches to as a mount point.

Raw disk

Although not technically a filesystem, vSphere also supports storing virtual machine guest files on a raw disk. This is configured by selecting **Raw Device Mapping** when adding a new virtual disk to a VM. In general, this allows a guest OS to utilize its preferred filesystem directly on the SAN. A **Raw Device Mapping (RDM)** may be mounted in a couple of different compatibility modes: physical or virtual. In physical mode, all commands except for REPORT LUNS are sent directly to the storage device. REPORT LUNS is masked in order to allow the VMkernel to isolate the LUN from the virtual machine. In virtual mode, only read and write commands are sent directly to the storage device while the VMkernel handles all other commands from the virtual machine. Virtual mode allows you to take advantage of many of vSphere's features such as file locking and snapshotting whereas physical mode does not.

The following table explains the supported storage connections in vSphere:

	Fibre Channel	FCoE	iSCSI	NFS
Description	Remote blocks are accessed by encapsulating SCSI commands and data into FC frames and transmitted over the FC network.	Remote blocks are accessed by encapsulating SCSI commands and data into Ethernet frames. FCoE contains many of the same characteristics as Fibre Channel except for Ethernet transport.	Remote blocks are accessed by encapsulating SCSI commands and data into TCP/IP packets and transmitted over the Ethernet network.	ESXi hosts access metadata and files located on the NFS server by utilizing file devices that are presented over a network.
Filesystem support	VMFS (block)	VMFS (block)	VMFS (block)	NFS (file)
Interface	Requires a dedicated **Host Bus Adapter (HBA)**.	Requires either a hardware converged network adapter or NIC that supports FCoE capabilities in conjunction with the built-in software FCoE initiator.	Requires either a dependent or independent hardware iSCSI initiator or a NIC with iSCSI capabilities utilizing the built-in software iSCSI initiator and a VMkernel port.	Requires a NIC and the use of a VMkernel port.

	Fibre Channel FCoE	iSCSI	NFS
Load Balancing/ Failover	Uses VMware's Pluggable Storage Architecture to provide standard path selections and failover mechanisms.	Utilizes VMware's Pluggable Storage Architecture as well as the built-in iSCSI binding functionality.	Due to the nature of NFS implementing a single session, there is no load balancing available. Aggregate bandwidth can be achieved by manually accessing the NFS server across different paths. Failover can be configured only in an active/ standby type configuration.
Security	Utilizes zoning between the hosts and the FC targets to isolate storage devices from hosts.	Utilizes **Challenge Handshake Authentication Protocol** (**CHAP**) to allow different hosts to see different LUNs.	Depends on the NFS storage device. Most implement an **access control list** (**ACL**) type deployment to allow hosts to see certain NFS exports.

Storage naming

In order to begin troubleshooting vSphere Storage, we need to be aware of how vSphere identifies and names the storage devices, LUNs, and paths available to our hosts. During the process of troubleshooting of vSphere Storage, there are a lot of situations where we need to provide the identifier of a storage device or path in order to obtain more information about the issue. Due to the uniqueness of these identifiers, ESXi will often use them when logging issues to syslog.

Viewing device identifiers

We are able to view device identifiers in a couple of different places; within the vSphere Client and within the ESXi Shell. Let us have a look at each in turn.

Within the vSphere Client

We can view the device identifiers within the vSphere Client by performing the following steps:

1. Click on the **Configuration** tab of the host whose storage you wish to view.

2. Click on the **Storage** section under **Hardware**.

3. Switch to the **Devices** view and right-click on the header bar to add and remove desired columns if needed.

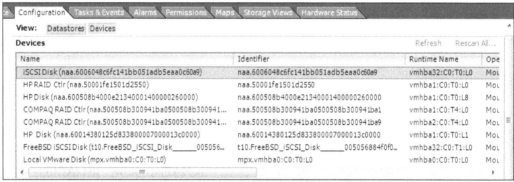

Device identifiers from the vSphere Client

Within ESXi Shell

The following command will give us similar information as to what we see in the vSphere Client and should return similar information to that of the following screenshot:

```
esxcfg-scsidevs -c
```

```
~ # esxcfg-scsidevs -c
Device UID                                                   Device Type      Console D
evice                                                                 Size     Multi
path PluginDisplay Name
mpx.vmhba0:C0:T0:L0                                          Direct-Access    /vmfs/dev
ices/disks/mpx.vmhba0:C0:T0:L0                                        69973MB    NMP
   Local VMware Disk (mpx.vmhba0:C0:T0:L0)
naa.50001fe1501d2550                                         RAID Ctlr        /vmfs/dev
ices/genscsi/naa.50001fe1501d2550                                    0MB        NMP
   HP RAID Ctlr (naa.50001fe1501d2550)
naa.500508b300941ba0500508b300941ba1                         RAID Ctlr        /vmfs/dev
ices/genscsi/naa.500508b300941ba0500508b300941ba1                    0MB        NMP
   COMPAQ RAID Ctlr (naa.500508b300941ba0500508b300941ba1)
naa.500508b300941ba0500508b300941ba9                         RAID Ctlr        /vmfs/dev
ices/genscsi/naa.500508b300941ba0500508b300941ba9                    0MB        NMP
   COMPAQ RAID Ctlr (naa.500508b300941ba0500508b300941ba9)
naa.60014380125d833800007000013c0000                         Direct-Access    /vmfs/dev
ices/disks/naa.60014380125d833800007000013c0000                      204800MB   NMP
   HP  Disk (naa.60014380125d833800007000013c0000)
naa.600508b4000e21340001400000260000                         Direct-Access    /vmfs/dev
ices/disks/naa.600508b4000e21340001400000260000                      102400MB   NMP
   HP Disk (naa.600508b4000e21340001400000260000)
naa.6006048c6fc141bb051adb5eaa0c60a9                         Direct-Access    /vmfs/dev
ices/disks/naa.6006048c6fc141bb051adb5eaa0c60a9                      102400MB   NMP
   iSCSI Disk (naa.6006048c6fc141bb051adb5eaa0c60a9)
t10.FreeBSD_iSCSI_Disk     005056884f0f000_____   Direct-Access    /vmfs/dev
ices/disks/t10.FreeBSD_iSCSI_Disk_____005056884f0f000             16384MB    NMP
   FreeBSD iSCSI Disk (t10.FreeBSD_iSCSI_Disk_____005056884f0f000_____)
```

Device identifiers from within the vSphere CLI

The many ways vSphere identifies storage

As shown in the previous two screenshots, we can see that there are three different identifiers as it pertains to storage naming: friendly names, identifiers, and runtime names.

Friendly names

Friendly names are generated by the host and can be modified and defined by the administrator.

Identifiers

Identifiers are not user definable due to the sheer fact that they must be unique and persistent in the case of a host reboot. Identifiers are displayed in one of many different formats which are derived depending on the storage subsystem presenting the device. In the previous two screenshots, you can see a variety of identifiers are used.

NAA identifiers

A large majority of storage devices return NAA identifiers which all begin with "naa.". An NAA identifier is often compared to that of a MAC address on a NIC as it is defined by certain standards and is always unique to the device being presented.

T10 identifiers

Another type of identifier shown is called a T10 identifier and always begins with "t10.". Normally, T10 identifiers are associated with an iSCSI array; however, it could be returned from any SCSI device. T10 identifiers are also governed by standards and like NAA identifiers, should always be unique.

IQN identifiers

Another identifier type which is solely used on iSCSI arrays is an **iSCSI Qualified Name (IQN)**. IQNs are normally user configurable on the iSCSI arrays which in turn does not guarantee uniqueness on a global scale, but we should always ensure we have uniqueness within our environment. IQNs will always begin with "iqn." and just like NAA and T10 identifiers, must be persistent across reboots. Even if your iSCSI array is using IQN, there are times when it will return a T10 identifier, or a mixture of T10 and IQN identifiers.

MPX identifiers

The last type of identifier we can see in the previous two screenshots is an MPX identifier. **MPX (VMware Multipath X Device)** identifiers are generated by the ESXi host when the device does not return a naa, T10, or IQN identifier, and always begin with "mpx.". Unlike the other industry standard identifiers, MPX is not globally unique and is not persistent during a reboot. Normally, MPX identifiers are only seen on devices such as a CD or DVD ROM as they usually do not respond with any industry standard identifier.

Runtime names

Runtime names basically describe the first path to the device as assigned by the host. Although these usually don't change, there is no guarantee that they will persist across reboots since we cannot guarantee that a certain path to a storage device will always be active. Runtime names are constructed using the format shown in the following table:

Format	Explanation
vmhba(N)	N will be the physical storage adapter in the ESXi host.
C(N)	It describes the channel number.
T(N)	It describes the target number as decided by the ESXi host. These are not guaranteed to be unique between hosts nor are they persistent across reboots.
L(N)	The LUN number as defined by the storage system.

As you can conclude from the above description, the device described in the previous two screenshots with the identifier naa.600508b400 0e21340001400000260000 exists on vmhba1, channel 0, target 0, and LUN 8, and therefore has a runtime name of vmhba1:C0:T0:L8.

Since friendly names are user definable and runtime names are not persistent across reboots or rescans, we will normally use the naa, t10, or IQN identifier when accessing and troubleshooting storage. It's the only form of storage naming that provides us the persistence and uniqueness that we need to ensure we are dealing with the proper datastore or path.

The vSphere Pluggable Storage Architecture

The vSphere Pluggable Storage Architecture is essentially a collection of plugins that reside inside the VMkernel layer of an ESXi host. The following figure shows a graphical representation of all the components of the PSA. The top-level plugin in the PSA is the **Multipathing Plugin** (**MPP**). The MPP defines how vSphere will manage and access storage including load balancing, path selection, and failover. The MPP itself can be provided by the storage vendor (IE EMC PowerPath) or you may also use the VMware provided **Native Multipathing Plugin** (**NMP**).

So essentially, the VMware provided NMP is in itself a MPP. The NMP is loaded by default for all storage devices, however, it can be overridden and replaced by installing a third-party MPP. Within each MPP, including the VMware NMP are two subplugins; **Storage Array Type Plugin** (**SATP**) and **Path Selection Plugin** (**PSP**). The SATP handles the details about path failover, whereas the PSP handles the details around load balancing and which physical path to use to issue an I/O request.

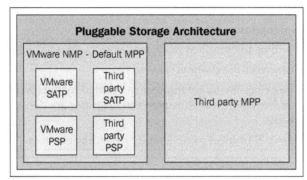

The VMware Pluggable Storage Architecture

Confused yet? I know the PSA is a lot to take in but it is essential to understand when you are troubleshooting storage issues. Let's have a look at each individual plugin included in the default VMware NMP in a little more detail to better understand the role it plays.

Pluggable Storage Architecture (PSA) roles and commands

The PSA performs two essential tasks as it pertains to storage:

- Discover which storage devices are available on a host
- Assign predefined claim rules associated with an MPP to take control of the storage device. Claim rules are explained in more detail in *Chapter 3, Troubleshooting Storage Visibility*.

In order to view a list of the PSA plugins, we use the `storage core` namespace of the `esxcli` command:

```
esxcli storage core plugin list
```

Multipathing Plugin – the VMware Native Multipathing Plugin roles and commands

The NMP/MPP performs the following functions:

- The MPP claims a physical path to the device, that is, SATP
- NMP comes with its own set of claim rules that associate certain SATP with a PSP
- Exports a logical device to the physical path contained in the PSP

To list devices controlled by the NMP with their respective SATP and PSP information, use the `storage nmp` namespace of `esxcli`, as outlined:

```
esxcli storage nmp device list
```

Storage Array Type Plugin roles and commands

The SATP plugin, which is a subplugin of the overall MPP, performs the following functions:

- Monitors the state of paths to the physical storage system
- Determines when a physical path is to be declared failed or down
- Handles the switching of physical paths after a path failure has occurred
- VMware provides a number of SATP plugins depending on which supported storage array is being used and also some generic active-active/active-passive SATP's for unknown storage arrays

To list the currently loaded SATP plugins along with their default PSP information, run the `storage nmp` namespace with `esxcli`.

```
esxcli storage nmp satp list
```

To change the default PSP associated with a given SATP, you can use the `esxcli storage nmp satp set -b <boottime> -P <Default PSP> -s <SATP>` command similar to the one shown in following screenshot:

```
~ # esxcli storage nmp satp set -P VMW_PSP_RR -s VMW_SATP_EVA
Default PSP for VMW_SATP_EVA is now VMW_PSP_RR
~ #
```

Associate a default PSP with a SATP via esxcli

Path Selection Plugin roles and commands

The PSP, which is a subplugin of the overall MPP, provides the PSA with the following functionality:

- Responsible for choosing a path to issue an I/O request.

- Differs from SATP in terms that the PSP is a load balancing mechanism and deals with only active paths. The SATP determines which paths are active/standby/failed.

- VMware provides three default PSP plugins; Fixed, Most Recently Used, and Round Robin.

- The VMware NMP will select a default PSP based on which SATP plugin has been loaded for the storage array.

To list all of the available PSP plugins, you can use the `storage nmp psp` namespace of `esxcli` as shown:

```
esxcli storage nmp psp list
```

More information in regards to each of the default policies that VMware provides is listed in the following table:

Policy	Explanation	Use
VMW_PSP_FIXED (Fixed)	Host uses a designated preferred path if configured; otherwise it uses the first available path at boot time. The host will failover to other paths if preferred path is down and will return to the initial preferred path when connection is restored	Default policy for most active-active arrays.
VMW_PSP_MRU (Most Recently Used)	Host will select the path that was used most recently. Upon failover, the host will move to another path. When the connection is restored, it will not revert back to the initial path.	Default policy for most active-passive arrays.
VMW_PSP_RR (Round Robin)	The host will cycle IOPs through all active paths on active-passive arrays and all paths on active-active arrays.	Default for a number of active-active and active-passive arrays.

To list certain configuration of the different PSP's on certain devices, you can use the `esxcli storage nmp psp <PSP Namespace> deviceconfig get -d <device identifier` command similar to the one shown in the following screenshot. On the flip side, you can set certain parameters by replacing `get` with `set`.

```
~ # esxcli storage nmp psp roundrobin deviceconfig get -d naa.600508b4000e21340001400000260000
  Byte Limit: 10485760
  Device: naa.600508b4000e21340001400000260000
  IOOperation Limit: 1000
  Limit Type: Default
  Use Active Unoptimized Paths: false
~ # 
```

Retrieving configuration from a devices PSP via esxcli

Although we have used the ESXi Shell to obtain all of the information mentioned previously, we should note that it is possible to retrieve and change some of the information from within the vSphere Client as well. Most of these operations are done in the **Storage** section of the **Configuration** tab of a host.

An I/O request – from start to finish

Now that we have a general understanding of how ESXi presents storage to a virtual machine and handles load balancing and failover, let's have a look at an I/O request from start to finish. The following figure shows a graphical representation of the following steps:

- The VM issues a SCSI request to its respective virtual disk.
- Drivers from within the guest OS communicate with the virtual storage adapters.
- The virtual storage adapter forwards the command to the VMkernel where the PSA takes over.
  - The PSA loads the specific MPP (in our case the NMP) depending on the logical device holding the virtual machines disk.
  - The NMP calls the associated PSP for the logical device
  - The PSP selects the appropriate path to send the I/O down while taking into consideration any load balancing techniques. The I/O is then queued to the hardware/software initiator, CNA, or HBA depending on the storage transport being used.
  - If the previous step fails, the NMP calls the appropriate SATP to process error codes and mark paths inactive or failed, and then the previous step is repeated.

- The hardware/software initiator, CNA, or FC HBA transforms the I/O request into the proper form depending on the storage transport (iSCSI, FC, or FCoE) and sends the request as per the PSAs instructions.

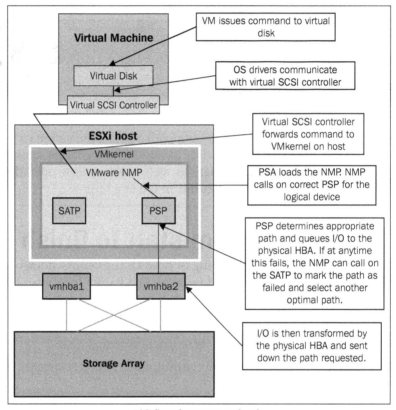

I/O flow from start to finish

Summary

We should now have a basic understanding of the common storage concepts, terms, methodologies, and transports that vSphere uses. We discussed the various types of storage that vSphere supports, including VMFS and NFS along with the many transports it utilizes to access these such as Fibre Channel and iSCSI. We went over how to identify storage LUNS, devices, and paths and have a basic understanding of the Pluggable Storage Architecture and how data flows from a virtualized application right through to its underlying storage.

In the next chapter, we will look at developing a proper troubleshooting methodology as well as review some of the most commonly used tools that can help us when troubleshooting vSphere storage.

2
Commonly Used Tools for Troubleshooting Storage

Now that we have established a little bit of background knowledge on some of the storage concepts and how to identify different components as it pertains to storage within vSphere, it's time to look at a few tools we can use to aid us in troubleshooting storage issues.

This chapter will give you basic knowledge of a troubleshooting methodology provided by VMware and then show us how we can use some of the built-in tools and logs from within vSphere, ESXi, and other applications to discover and solve storage issues. This fundamental knowledge of how to use these tools is key to understanding and interpreting some of the examples throughout the book.

This chapter will cover the following:

- The vSphere troubleshooting methodology
- Using vCenter Storage Maps and Storage Reports
- Using `esxtop`/`resxtop`
- Common logfiles used in storage troubleshooting

The vSphere troubleshooting methodology

In February 2011, VMware released a technical whitepaper titled *Performance Troubleshooting for vSphere 4.1* available at http://www.vmware.com/resources/techresources/10179. This document provides a large quantity of information as it pertains to troubleshooting not just storage but also CPU, memory, and network from within a vSphere environment and I highly recommend you read it for yourself. Although the current version of vSphere has changed since its publication, the methodologies, workflows, and recommendations in the document still stand today.

That being said, I will highlight some of the key points of the document as well as explain the importance of applying a troubleshooting methodology within our own environments.

When developing any type of process or workflow, it is very important to start with a broad and holistic view of the overall goal, and the same holds true with a troubleshooting methodology. Although you may find as you move through the process of creating your own or modifying an existing troubleshooting methodology that some elements may require their own subprocesses, it is still best to start with that broad overall look at your environment.

Why? Well, quite often when a problem or an issue arises, be it a vSphere environment or not, administrators will often begin troubleshooting issues in response to the first item they see in a log or an error message that has been displayed. At times this is ok; however, sometimes issues tend to be the result of another issue located somewhere down the stack.

Take for an instance, a VM failing to power on. There are a variety of reasons that VM could fail to power on. Some of them are as follows:

- The datastore it resides in may be full and the host may not be able to create a swapfile for the VM
- Another host could have a lock placed on the metadata for that VM
- High Availability admission control could prevent a VM from powering on
- The underlying storage may not be accessible
- The VM's configuration file may be corrupt or inaccessible

These are just a few examples of root causes and as you can see focusing our efforts on one single component could result in a lot of time wasted and a violation of SLAs. The process of looking at the issues on a large scale and the elimination of different components in the environment is the key to creating an efficient methodology that will result in us finding the root cause of the issue as fast as possible.

As stated in the document, we need to start with what's called a **top-level troubleshooting flow**. The purpose of this is to do a number of things:

- Identifies success criteria (how do we know when we are done or the issue has been solved)

- Points us to the various places where we can go to get more information about the problem

- Gives us direction on how to perform basic troubleshooting of the issue to further pinpoint the root cause (mainly covering common issues)

- Provides us with subprocesses or an advanced type of troubleshooting in case the issue isn't pinpointed and solved within the basic realm

For most of the part, we will be going through the troubleshooting process more than the design process so it is absolutely important that we are aware of the steps we need to take during the troubleshooting process and that they are well documented. *Appendix A, Troubleshooting Steps*, gives us a great example of how we can start with a large issue and narrow it down piece by piece.

Throughout the rest of this chapter, we will go through some of the tools and applications included with vSphere that you may want to include within your own troubleshooting methodology for vSphere Storage.

vCenter Storage Views (Reports and Maps)

One of the most commonly used tools used to troubleshoot storage is the **Storage Views** tab inside the vSphere Client. These storage views provide us with an easy and efficient way to determine what is consuming all of our storage as well as giving us a visually appealing graphical representation of how all of our inventory objects are connected as it pertains to storage.

Storage views should be available by default within the vSphere Client; however, I have seen times when the tab is not displayed. The storage views functionality is provided by a plugin within vSphere so if you don't see it be sure to have a look in your plugin manager for the vCenter Storage Monitoring plugin and make sure that it is enabled.

The **Storage Views** tab is available on three of the four vCenter Server Inventory layouts; **Hosts & Clusters**, **VMs and Templates**, and **Datastores**. Depending on which inventory object is selected, the data being displayed will change. However, one thing that is consistent no matter which inventory objects we have selected, we will always see two different layouts inside **Storage Views**; **Reports** and **Maps**.

Reports

The **Reports** view is a very powerful tool, especially when looking to view all the information about a specific object in one place. The first item to take note on the Reports storage view is the drop-down selection box in the top left hand corner (**Show All ...**). Using this box, you are able to quickly switch between a variety of views containing information about your VMs, SCSI paths, datastores, and even the physical HBA's contained in the hosts.

The following screenshot displays an example of a view using **Show All Virtual Machines**. You can see how the information displayed by default can be invaluable when troubleshooting vSphere Storage. First of all, we are able to see and view the capacity that a VM is occupying with regards to snapshot space.

> Snapshots will be explained a bit further in *Chapter 5, Troubleshooting Storage Capacity and Overcommitment*, but the point is that over time, snapshots can grow to be very large and we not only take an I/O hit but also risk the chance of filling up a datastore which usually results in outages.

Storage view reports are a great way to view just how much snapshot space any VMs are using. That being said, what is displayed by default is not all that has been collected. If we right-click along the column header, we can see that there are many other columns that can be added and removed from the report, which can be resized, reordered, and sorted in any manner we prefer.

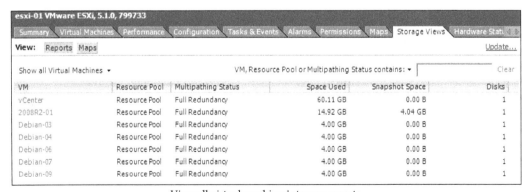

VM	Resource Pool	Multipathing Status	Space Used	Snapshot Space	Disks
vCenter	Resource Pool	Full Redundancy	60.11 GB	0.00 B	1
2008R2-01	Resource Pool	Full Redundancy	14.92 GB	4.04 GB	1
Debian-03	Resource Pool	Full Redundancy	4.00 GB	0.00 B	1
Debian-04	Resource Pool	Full Redundancy	4.00 GB	0.00 B	1
Debian-06	Resource Pool	Full Redundancy	4.00 GB	0.00 B	1
Debian-07	Resource Pool	Full Redundancy	4.00 GB	0.00 B	1
Debian-09	Resource Pool	Full Redundancy	4.00 GB	0.00 B	1

View all virtual machines' storage reports

Do you need to export the data you see on a storage report? Simply right-click anywhere inside your report and select **Export List**. Storage reports can be exported to a variety of formats including HTML, XLS, CSV, and XML.

Another way storage reports can aid in troubleshooting storage is using multipathing. By filtering our view to **Show All Datastores**, we can quickly see our path redundancy under the `Multipathing Status` column (following screenshot). It gives us a nice overview of the redundancy status of all of our datastores.

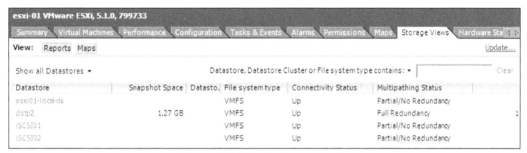

Show all datastore's storage reports

To view the paths associated with a datastore, we can simply click on the datastore name and the report will automatically switch to the Datastores context. To examine paths and their status, we can now switch to **Show all SCSI paths** and view the `Status` column (the following screenshot) to quickly see what is up and what is down as it pertains to the paths to our storage.

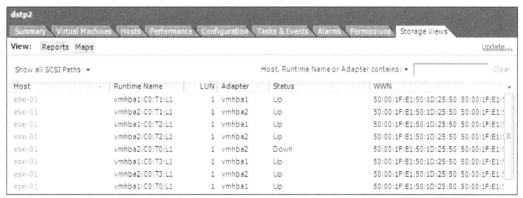

Show all SCSI paths' storage report

You can filter any column using the filter box on the top right-hand corner. Simply select the column you would like to filter from by selecting the down arrow and type in your expression in the filter box.

As you can see storage view reports can be a very powerful tool when it comes to troubleshooting storage. Having all this information inside one tab is certainly beneficial and really helps when we are looking for any **obvious** issues inside our environment. Certainly this is one of the first places I go to when troubleshooting any storage issues.

Maps

The **Maps** section in the **Storage Views** tab builds off where the standard datastore maps left off. It means we have all the information that datastore maps had, along with a little bit extra. Essentially, the mapping functionality provides us with a graphical representation of how our ESXi hosts and VMs are connected and intertwined to our storage.

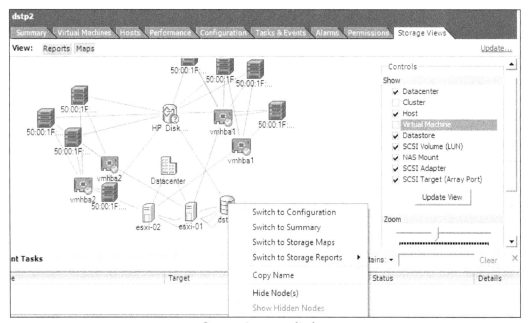

Storage view maps display

While we may not always use the **Maps** view in our troubleshooting, it does provide some interesting and quick navigational shortcuts when moving around in the vSphere Client. Say for instance, you were mapping out how your ESXi hosts are connected to your datastores as in the preceding screenshot. By right-clicking on any object on the map, you will see a **Switch to** option in the context menu. This is a quick and easy way to get to the configuration or summary pages of the items in question.

 Maps can also be exported to a variety of images files as well as a Visio compatible EMF file.

Using esxtop/resxtop

VMware's `esxtop` command is a very useful tool when it comes to really understanding and troubleshooting our environment. For anyone who has ever used the Linux's `top` command, you will notice that it is very similar in functionality and usability; however, the difference is that `esxtop` is only available within the ESXi command-line interface (with the exception of `resxtop`, which is available from the vSphere Management Assistant) and is geared towards a virtual environment. The `esxtop` tool provides us with many real-time statistics with regard to how our virtual environment is utilizing resources and performing.

However, `esxtop` is not just a storage troubleshooting tool. We can see in the following screenshot that `esxtop` is able to present displays on CPU, memory, network, power, interrupt, disk adapters, disk devices, and individual virtual machine disks. For the scope of this book, we will cover only the storage related displays of `esxtop`; however, I highly recommend reading up on all the displays available.

 We can adjust the display within `esxtop` by pressing *h* to present the different views and their corresponding navigation characters.

`esxtop` will be referenced frequently in the upcoming chapters of this book, so it is imperative that we learn how to navigate through the tools interface, switch to different displays, modify refresh rates, and customize field displays. The statistics that are collected as well as their respective thresholds, along with all the interactive commands are explained in detail in *Appendix B, Statistics of esxtop*. For now, we will just learn the basic navigation and customizations available in the tool.

esxtop always displays data in real-time which means it's impossible to go back and review data from the past. If you are experiencing issues at a certain time, it's possible to schedule and run esxtop in batch mode in order to capture different statistics at a certain point in time. This data is then saved to a CSV file for further analysis. For more information on batch mode, see *Appendix B, Statistics of esxtop*.

Switching displays

Switching to the different displays within esxtop is very easy. As shown in the following screenshot, we can switch to a desired display by hitting the shortcut key which is shown on the left-hand side of the display. So, press *d* for disk adapter, *u* for disk device, *v* for disk VM, and so on.

```
space    - update display
h or ?   - help; show this text
q        - quit

Interactive commands are:

fF       Add or remove fields
oO       Change the order of displayed fields
s        Set the delay in seconds between updates
#        Set the number of instances to display
W        Write configuration file ~/.esxtop50rc
k        Kill a world
e        Expand/Rollup Cpu Statistics
V        View only VM instances
L        Change the length of the NAME field
l        Limit display to a single group

Sort by:
        U:%USED          R:%RDY          N:GID
Switch display:
        c:cpu            i:interrupt     m:memory        n:network
        d:disk adapter   u:disk device   v:disk VM       p:power mgmt

Hit any key to continue:
```

esxtop help screen

Field customization

Each display will provide us with a number of different statistics by default and just as we can do inside **Storage Views**, we have the power to hide or unhide different columns. To do so in `esxtop`, just press the *f* key when on the display screen. We will now be presented with the **Field Order** screen as shown in the following screenshot.

To toggle whether fields are displayed or not, simply press the corresponding key and an asterisk should either appear or disappear marking the field as displayed or not.

```
Current Field order: ABCdEfGhijkl

* A:  ADAPTR = Adapter Name
* B:  PATH = Path Name
* C:  NPATHS = Num Paths
  D:  QSTATS = Queue Stats
* E:  IOSTATS = I/O Stats
  F:  RESVSTATS = Reserve Stats
* G:  LATSTATS/cmd = Overall Latency Stats (ms)
  H:  LATSTATS/rd = Read Latency Stats (ms)
  I:  LATSTATS/wr = Write Latency Stats (ms)
  J:  ERRSTATS/s = Error Stats
  K:  PAESTATS/s = PAE Stats
  L:  SPLTSTATS/s = SPLIT Stats

Toggle fields with a-l, any other key to return: █
```

esxtop field selection screen

The default order in which columns are displayed can also be changed. This is done by pressing the *o* key. Once on the **Field Order** screen, you can either move a field left and right by pressing either the uppercase or lowercase keys that corresponds with the field. Uppercase is used for moving the field left and lowercase is used for moving the field right.

Some data is also rolled up within `esxtop`. For instance, when looking at the **Disk Adapter** display, all of the statistics will be rolled up by the adapter name and presented in a manner of vmhba1, vmhba2, and so on. What isn't really clear here is that we are actually displaying the aggregated data from all paths on each HBA. To expand this further, press the *e* key and enter the desired adapter name.

We can now see in the following screenshot all of statistics segregated out by path for vmhba2.

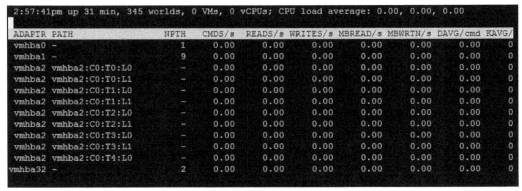

ADAPTR	PATH	NPTH	CMDS/s	READS/s	WRITES/s	MBREAD/s	MBWRTN/s	DAVG/cmd	KAVG/
vmhba0	-	1	0.00	0.00	0.00	0.00	0.00	0.00	0
vmhba1	-	9	0.00	0.00	0.00	0.00	0.00	0.00	0
vmhba2	vmhba2:C0:T0:L0	-	0.00	0.00	0.00	0.00	0.00	0.00	0
vmhba2	vmhba2:C0:T0:L1	-	0.00	0.00	0.00	0.00	0.00	0.00	0
vmhba2	vmhba2:C0:T1:L0	-	0.00	0.00	0.00	0.00	0.00	0.00	0
vmhba2	vmhba2:C0:T1:L1	-	0.00	0.00	0.00	0.00	0.00	0.00	0
vmhba2	vmhba2:C0:T2:L0	-	0.00	0.00	0.00	0.00	0.00	0.00	0
vmhba2	vmhba2:C0:T2:L1	-	0.00	0.00	0.00	0.00	0.00	0.00	0
vmhba2	vmhba2:C0:T3:L0	-	0.00	0.00	0.00	0.00	0.00	0.00	0
vmhba2	vmhba2:C0:T3:L1	-	0.00	0.00	0.00	0.00	0.00	0.00	0
vmhba2	vmhba2:C0:T4:L0	-	0.00	0.00	0.00	0.00	0.00	0.00	0
vmhba32	-	2	0.00	0.00	0.00	0.00	0.00	0.00	0

esxtop expanded statistics

 We can also limit the amount of rows returned by esxtop by pressing the # key and the desired number of rows. This can come in handy when only looking to view the top two LUNs as it pertains to latency, aborts, and so on.

Refresh interval

By default, esxtop will refresh the data being displayed every 5 seconds. 5 seconds might not seem that long in real life; however, in the computing industry when dealing with troubleshooting, it may seem like a lifetime. The refresh interval can be changed by pressing *s* and then the desired number in seconds.

Logfiles used in vSphere Storage troubleshooting

Logfiles have long been the norm for providing us with a wealth of information as to what is occurring inside any system. The same holds true with vSphere and ESXi. In fact, vSphere has quite a few logfiles that it uses to report on almost every single event that occurs within our environment. This is the main reason why the first thing that is asked to any customer during a support call is to send the logfile bundle for further analysis. Whether it is the ESXi host, vCenter Server, or the virtual machine itself, each has its own set of logfiles stored in different locations.

ESXi logging

ESXi has a very robust logging system with a number of different logfiles. Each one provides a unique and organized way of logging different events that occur. For instance, shell authentication events go to the `auth` log, patch and update events will go to the `esxupdate` log, and so on. The following table shows a full list of all the logs contained in an ESXi host and a description of what they are mainly used for:

Log location	Description
/var/log/auth.log	ESXi Shell authentication messages (successes and failures).
/var/log/dhclient.log	DHCP client service information.
/var/log/esxupdate.log	Path and update information.
/var/log/hostd.log	Host management information, including all virtual machine and host task and events, communication with the vSphere Client, vCenter Server vpxa agent, and all SDK connections
/var/log/shell.log	ESXi Shell Usage History—includes all commands executed while in the ESXi Shell.
/var/log/sysboot.log	Early VMkernel start-up and module loading.
/var/log/syslog.log	Management service initialization, watchdogs, and scheduled task information. Also included usage information of the **Direct User Console Interface (DUCI)**.
/var/log/usb.log	Information as it pertains to discovery and pass-through configuration of USB devices.
/var/log/vob.log	VMkernel observation events.
/var/log/vmkernel.log	Core VMkernel information, including all device discovery, storage, networking device events, and virtual machine startup,
/var/log/vmkwarning.log	Summary of warning and alert events from the VMkernel logs.
/var/log/vmksummary.log	Summary of ESXi host start-up and shutdown events, along with heartbeat information, virtual machine running information, and service resource consumption.

Certainly we do not need to use all of these logs when it comes to troubleshooting storage. Throughout this book, however, you will see reference to a few; mainly the `sysboot.log`, `vmkernel.log`, and `hostd.log` files as these files contain the most crucial storage events that ESXi logs.

Most of the storage logging in ESXi is enabled by default; however, there are some things that are not. Look for parameters starting with SCSI. Log in the hosts advanced settings to see what is enabled and what is not. Simply toggling these values from 1 or 0 turns them on and off.

Viewing ESXi logs

There are a few different ways to view the logs on an ESXi host. One of the most common that I use is directly accessing the files through the command-line interface. The ESXi shell runs a BusyBox console which includes a lot of the Linux commands that you would normally use such as grep, cat, tail, more, and less. These commands are invaluable when searching through logs. Could you imagine trying to read thousands of log entries inside notepad?

Below are a few different variations of these commands which we will see throughout the book that can definitely help us identify and troubleshoot issues more efficiently when it comes to reading logfiles.

To search through an individual file for a specified search term, use the following command:

```
grep -r search_term /var/log/vmkernel.log
```

Use the following command to search through all logs inside /var/log recursively for a specified search term. The results of this command will contain every single line that contains the search criteria:

```
grep -r search_term /var/log/*
```

To perform the same search as done previously but returning not only the line that contains the search term but also the three lines above it and two lines below it as well, use the following command:

```
grep -r -A3 -B2 search_term /var/log/*
```

To search through vmkernel.log for all occurrences of SCSI and Failed on the same line, use the following command:

```
cat /var/log/vmkernel.log | grep SCSI | grep -i Failed
```

> If these commands are returning too many results and filling up your console session, try adding a "| less" to the end of the command to pause the output when your screen is full. This allows you to move up and down and search through the results.
>
> ```
> cat /var/log/vmkernel.log | grep -i SCSI | less
> ```

To view the last ten entries in the `hostd.log` file, use the following command:

```
tail -n10 /var/log/hostd.log
```

To view the first ten entries in the `hostd.log` file, use the following command:

```
head -n10 /var/log/hostd.log
```

To watch (follow) the `vmkwarning.log` file as new entries are written to the file, use the following command:

```
tail -f /var/log/vmkwarning.log
```

> Not comfortable with ESXi command line? No problem! There are many other ways to view the ESXi logs, such as:
>
> * Through the **View System Logs** option on the DCUI
> * Through a web browser by browsing to `https://IPAddress/host` and authenticating.
> * Using the `vifs` command-line utility from the vSphere Management Assistant.
> * Through the **File | Export Logs** functionality in the vSphere Client.

vCenter Server logging

Although vCenter Server logs are not primarily used for storage troubleshooting, it's still a good practice to know where they are located and the general information that is stored inside them. The vSphere infrastructure is very intertwined when it comes to compute, memory, networking, management, and storage; so one issue that appears to be storage related could actually have a root cause that is management related.

The following tables describe where the vCenter Server logs are located and what is actually logged to each file:

vCenter Server instance	Location of logfiles
vCenter Server running on Windows 2003 and earlier	`%ALLUSERSPROFILE%\ Application Data\VMware\VMware VirtualCenter\Logs\`
vCenter Server running on Windows 2008 and later	`C:\ProgramData\VMware\VMware VirtualCenter\Logs\`
vCenter Server Linux Virtual Appliance	`/var/log/vmware/vpx/`
vCenter Server Linux Virtual Appliance UI	`/var/log/vmware/vami/`

The following table shows vCenter Server logfile descriptions:

Logfile	Description
`vpxd.log`	Main vCenter Server log which contains all client and web service connections. All internal task and communication with the vpxa (vCenter Agent that runs on ESXi host) is also logged here.
`vpxd-profiler.log, profiler.log, scoreboard.log`	Profiled metrics for operations that vCenter performs in conjunction with the VOD.
`cim-diag.log, vws.log`	All **Common Information Modeling** (**CIM**) monitoring information. All information between the vCenter Server and the ESXi hosts CIM interface is logged here.
`drmdump\`	All actions that have been recommended and applied by the VMware **Distributed Resource Scheduler** (**DRS**) are logged here.

The vCenter Syslog Collector is an additional tool that is bundled with the vCenter Server media and can be used to have your ESXi hosts to ship their logs to vCenter Server. When possible, it's always a good practice to have a syslog server somewhere within your environment in the case that the original logs are not available. VMware has an excellent knowledge base article located at `http://kb.vmware.com/selfservice/microsites/search.do?language=en_US&cmd=displayKC&externalId=2003322` which explains how to configure syslog on ESXi.

Virtual machine logging

The third type of logging that is performed by vSphere is virtual machine logging. The virtual machine log is a file named `vmware.log` (by default) which is normally stored in the same folder as the virtual machines configuration (vmx) file. The virtual machine log becomes increasingly important when troubleshooting issues that are more tied to the virtual machine and how its virtual hardware is performing.

The `vmware.log` file contains all the information on how the VM is configured, actions that have been performed on it, and what virtual hardware is attached to it. This can also be an invaluable resource when troubleshooting Storage DRS, Storage vMotion, and Snapshots and for completely rebuilding a VMs configuration as it will contain a wide variety of information and clues as to what happened to a VM when a failure occurred.

> VMware has just released a new product called vCenter Log Insight which can provide end users with a powerful log analytics tool to search through not only the logfiles we just covered, but logfiles from other VMware products as well. It gives you the ability to use predefined dashboard-like pages or you can create your own dashboard-like pages to visually represent the data that is being reported in logs. More information on vCenter Log Insight can be found on the product page located at `http://www.vmware.com/products/vcenter-log-insight/`.

Summary

We should now have a good idea about some of the tools we can use to troubleshoot vSphere Storage, including Storage Maps/Reports, esxtop, and some of the common logfiles that vCenter and ESXi log information messages to. We should also note the importance of implementing and having a solid understanding of how to create and use a troubleshooting methodology within our own environments.

In the next chapter, we will use the knowledge and tools gained from the previous chapters to troubleshoot issues as they pertain to storage connectivity and visibility.

3
Troubleshooting Storage Visibility

Now that we have a solid understanding of how vSphere handles storage as well as a lot of the common tools we can use to troubleshoot and view storage, it's time to dive deep into the primary topic of this book which is troubleshooting vSphere Storage. In this chapter, we will walk through some of the common troubleshooting steps to take when LUNs are not visible to our ESXi hosts. We will also cover how to troubleshoot individual Fibre Channel paths to storage, storage claim rules, and LUN masking, as well as the process of resignaturing a LUN.

From there, we will move into IP storage and discuss the various troubleshooting steps to undertake when dealing with both iSCSI and NFS visibility issues.

This chapter covers the following:

- Common storage visibility issues across block transport types
  - ESXi claim rules and **Logical Unit Number** (**LUN**) masking
  - Troubleshooting paths and path selection
  - vCenter Server Storage filters
  - Disk resignaturing
  - LUN numbering
- Troubleshooting Fibre Channel storage visibility
  - Fibre Channel switch zoning
  - **Registered State Change Notifications** (**RSCN**)
  - Identifying and interpreting Fibre Channel connection issues in the logs

- Troubleshooting IP storage visibility
  - Verifying network connectivity to your iSCSI/NFS array
  - iSCSI and NFS port requirements
  - **Challenge Handshake Authentication Protocol (CHAP)** authentication
  - Identifying and interpreting iSCSI connection issues in the logs
  - Troubleshooting **Network File System** (**NFS**) storage
  - Identifying and interpreting NFS connection issues in the logs

Common storage visibility issues across block transport types

Both Fibre Channel and iSCSI use VMFS-formatted block storage as their data structure. Due to the commonalities of both storage transports, a lot of the steps you can take to troubleshoot connectivity and visibility issues overlap and are explained in the following sections.

ESXi claim rules and LUN masking

As we discussed in *Chapter 1*, *Understanding vSphere Storage Concepts and Methodologies*, each storage device managed by vSphere is connected by loading a plugin inside the **Pluggable Storage Architecture** (**PSA**). The process inside PSA that associates our storage array devices with the proper storage plugins, whether that is the default NMP provided by VMware or a third-party plugin provided by our storage vendor, is called **claiming**. Claiming is essentially a group of rules called **claim rules** that contain associations between the storage devices and either the MPP or the NMP.

So why are claim rules important when it comes to troubleshooting vSphere Storage visibility? Well, similar to Fibre Channel zoning and how it can block an ESXi host from having access to storage, claim rules can utilize what is called a **MASK_PATH** plugin to emulate the same functionality. Most commonly, these per-LUN masking techniques are done directly on the storage processor of your SAN; however, ESXi does have this technology implemented within its own stack.

Claim rules, along with the MASK_PATH plugin, can be loaded into runtime of the ESXi host in order to remove visibility to a certain LUN or a single path to a LUN.

Claim rules access is currently not available inside any of the vSphere clients. They can only be defined from within the ESXi **Command-Line Interface (CLI)**.

To list out the claim rules currently loaded, we can use the `esxcli storage core claimrule list` command as shown in the following screenshot.

```
~ # esxcli storage core claimrule list
Rule Class   Rule  Class    Type       Plugin      Matches
---------    ----  -------  ---------  ---------   ------------------------------------------
MP              0  runtime  transport  NMP         transport=usb
MP              1  runtime  transport  NMP         transport=sata
MP              2  runtime  transport  NMP         transport=ide
MP              3  runtime  transport  NMP         transport=block
MP              4  runtime  transport  NMP         transport=unknown
MP            101  runtime  vendor     MASK_PATH   vendor=DELL model=Universal Xport
MP            101  file     vendor     MASK_PATH   vendor=DELL model=Universal Xport
MP            400  runtime  location   MASK_PATH   adapter=vmhba32 channel=* target=1 lun=0
MP            400  file     location   MASK_PATH   adapter=vmhba32 channel=* target=1 lun=0
MP          65535  runtime  vendor     NMP         vendor=* model=*
~ #
```

Claimrule list

As illustrated in the preceding screenshot, claim rules have a required property called **Type**. The available types in vSphere are vendor, location, transport, and driver. A claim rule type defines the category of matching we wish to use for the claiming operation. We can apply the type "vendor" to match a specific vendor such as HP or EMC, the type "transport" to match a specific storage transport like iSCSI or Fibre Channel, the type "location" allows us to match a specific adapter or individual path, and the type "driver" applies our rules to specific drivers.

Another notable property of a claim rule is its ID (shown under the `Rule` column in the preceding screenshot). Every claim rule must be assigned an ID between `1` and `65534`. The highest claim rule ID is actually `65535`; however, this is reserved as a catch-all rule to allow vSphere to claim any device that does not get claimed by any previous rules in order for it to be managed by the NMP. Along with `65535`, `0-100` and `65436-65535` are also reserved by VMware for internal use.

Also when dealing with claim rules, another property to pay particular attention to is class. Class can be two types; file or runtime. File essentially means that the claim rule has been loaded into the system, whereas runtime defines that the claim rule is currently active and effective.

> Claim rules are executed in sequential order from smallest to largest with the largest ID overriding any conflicting rules. It means if you have a MASK_PATH definition at number 134, then a MPP claim at number 140, and another MPP claim at number 150 — the path will never be seen by vSphere as it will be masked and the MPP claim at 150 will take precedence over the one listed at 140.

While claim rules can be tedious to analyze, it is important to check them when troubleshooting storage connectivity issues in vSphere to ensure MASK_PATH is not causing the issue. Administrators may have masked away a complete storage array or certain individual paths during an upgrade or maintenance. So what do we do if we have a claim rule that is causing the issue? If we look at the claim rules listed in the previous screenshot, we can see that we have the **MASK_PATH** plugin loaded for LUN 0 on **vmhba32**. If we were trying to access the datastore on this LUN, we would need to remove the claim rule before our vSphere host would be able to discover it. Taking into account the information displayed in the previous screenshot, we could remove the rule with the following command:

```
esxcli storage core claimrule remove -rule 400
```

> Use caution when deleting claim rules as they aren't always as they appear. You may think you are solving an issue and end up creating another. Definitely take extra caution in any production environment and always run the vm-support command to dump your configuration before removing any claim rules in the event VMware support needs this information.

Please note that running a `remove` command will only remove the "file" class from the claim rule, not the runtime rule. In order for our removal to take effect, we will need to first load our current `claimrule` set with the following command:

```
esxcli storage core claimrule load
```

Secondly, we will need to unclaim the device or target in question from the MASK_PATH plugin. Again, using the information in the previous screenshot, we can unclaim our LUN with the following command:

```
esxcli storage core claiming unclaim -t location -A vmhba32 -T 1 -L 0
```

Only after reloading and unclaiming will the claim rule be completely removed from the ESXi host. A simple rescan of the HBA should now allow the host to see the datastore.

When troubleshooting storage inside vSphere, you should always perform a storage rescan after making changes. A lot of times our changes will not be reflected until a rescan of the HBA's have been performed. To do so, right-click on a host/cluster and select **Rescan for datastores**.

Troubleshooting paths and path selection

Whether it is the result of zoning, LUN masking, or other environmental issues, a dead or inactive path can definitely result in a datastore not showing up within vSphere if the proper redundancy design has not been implemented. Most Fibre Channel and iSCSI SANs today have at least two storage processors, allowing redundant links on the storage array to be present. In the event that one path fails, the other path can be activated depending on the failover method implemented.

In most cases, there will be at least two paths to the storage, more commonly we see 8 or 16 paths depending on the number of storage processors, HBAs (or initiators), and ports available. vSphere manages these paths using the PSA and more so the **Storage Array Type Plug-in (SATP)** and **Path Selection Policy (PSP)** associated with the storage array. This is why we need to pay attention to the PSP assigned to each array.

Although vSphere provides a default PSP for different SAN configurations (IE Active-Active SANs use Fixed, Active-Passive SANs use Most Recently Used); there are times when these will need to be changed. Storage vendors know best how their hardware will integrate with vSphere, so you should always check their recommendations and best practices. For instance, the HP MSA 1500cs has an Active-Active firmware, which in terms of VMware would be best suited with a Fixed PSP. That being said, most HP best practice articles recommend utilizing the Most Recently Used setting due to the nature of how the HP controllers handle the ownership and presentation of LUNS to ESXi. It is very important that we always check our storage vendor's recommendations and best practices when implementing vSphere Storage to ensure we are taking the best steps for performance and availability.

Another factor that can play a key role in vSphere Storage visibility is path states. It is no surprise that we repeatedly suggest that storage environments within vSphere are designed with redundancy in mind, allowing individual paths to fail and recover without affecting our production workloads. This is why it is important that we know how to view, configure, and monitor a path's state in order to pro-actively prevent outages and loss of data within our environments.

Examples of a path state include active, standby, dead, or disabled and basically describe the current flow of data through the path. To view the current state of a LUN's path inside of the vSphere Client, follow the following steps:

1. Select the host, Click on **Configuration** and select **Storage**.

2. Select the datastore and then click **Properties**.

3. Click on **Manage Paths**.

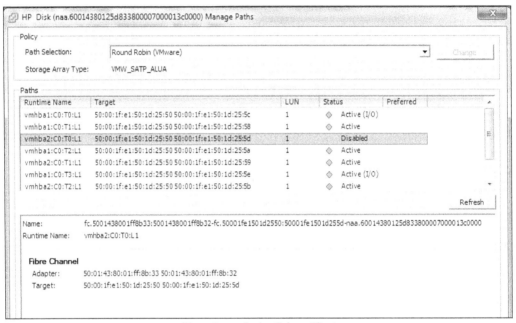

Managing paths in vSphere Client

We should now see the output similar to that of the preceding screenshot. In the **Manage Paths** screen, we are able to change the PSP associated with the LUN as well as disable/enable paths and mark paths as preferred if applicable.

Similarly, to check via CLI, we can use the `esxcli storage core path list` command which will list out all the available paths in the system. Adding a `-d` parameter and the device identifier will further limit our result to a specific device. From this, we can see the path status and how all of our LUNs are configured in terms of their PSP, but it is not very helpful in terms of actively monitoring the paths for a state change. We don't want to have to go into these screens every day to see if something has changed.

In order to take a proactive approach to a changed path state, we can set up an alarm within vCenter to monitor for a couple of different events; **Lost Storage Path Redundancy** and **Degraded Storage Path Redundancy**. The alarms are very similar in nature. Degraded Storage Path Redundancy will report on any path failure whereas Lost Storage Redundancy will only trigger when a LUN has no redundant paths left. The following screenshot shows us a triggered **Degraded Storage Path Redundancy** alarm. The steps to set up the alarms are as follows:

1. Click on your desired object to create the alarm and select the **Alarms** tab. In our case, we should have a host or cluster selected.

2. Click on the **Definitions** view and right-click anywhere within the blank space and select **New Alarm**.

3. Set the **Monitor** dropdown in the **Alarm** Type section to **Hosts**.

4. Select the option **Monitor for specific events occurring on this object, for example, VM powered on**.

5. In the **Triggers** tab, click on **Add**.

6. From the drop-down menu, select either **Lost Storage Path Redundancy** or **Degraded Storage Path Redundancy** depending on the type of alarm you want to set up.

7. If you wish to add any alerting functionality such as emails or SNMP traps, you can do so in the **Actions** tab. When done, click on **OK**.

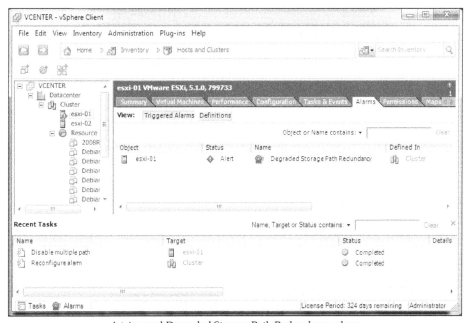

A triggered Degraded Storage Path Redundancy alarm

As shown in the preceding screenshot, vCenter alarms will alert us visually inside vSphere Client when problems occur. The host gets labeled with a red exclamation mark and a triggered alarm will show up within the **Alarms** tab when a down path is detected. We can even set up these alarms to send us notifications via e-mail or report to another monitoring solution you may have in place by sending an SNMP trap. It's recommended to use a combination of new and already built-in alarms in vSphere to proactively monitor your environment to help you in the troubleshooting process and alert you of any issues that are occurring before they turn into outages.

vCenter Server Storage filters

Another component of vSphere that will cause headaches when dealing with storage connectivity and visibility are vCenter Server Storage filters. vCenter Storage filters provide us with a way to filter out LUNs which meet a certain criteria. vCenter has four storage filters: VMFS Filter, RDM Filter, Same Host and Transports Filter, and Host Rescan Filter. These filters are all enabled by default and the details of the functionality they provide is listed in the following table:

Filter name	Filter key	Description
VMFS Filter	`config.vpxd.filter.vmfsFilter`	Filters out LUNs that already contain a VMFS partition
RDM Filter	`config.vpxd.filter.rdmFilter`	Filters out LUNs that have already been mapped inside vSphere as an RDM, whether it be in physical or virtual compatibility mode
Same Host and Transports Filter	`config.vpxd.filter.SameHostAndTransportsFilter`	Filters out LUNs that cannot be used as a datastore extent, that is, those LUNs that are not presented to all hosts or LUNs that may use a different storage type as the primary datastore extent.
Host Rescan Filter	`config.vpxd.filter.hostRescanFilter`	Automatically scans and updates datastores after any datastore operation is performed.

Apart from Host Rescan Filter, the other filters do just as they describe; filter out LUNs. Although these filters are in place to protect us from inadvertently destroying or corrupting data, sometimes they introduce troubles when we actually have a legitimate reason to see the LUNs that are being filtered. Take for instance setting up a Microsoft Cluster inside vSphere. In order to do so, we need to map the same raw LUN or RDM to all virtual machines participating in the cluster. With the RDM Filter running under its default configuration, only the host which is running the first VM to see the RDM would see this storage, and storage filters would filter that RDM on all other hosts. This is certainly a valid scenario where we would need to disable the RDM Filter in order to gain visibility to the LUN from other VMs on other hosts.

The storage filter settings are all contained inside the advanced vCenter Server settings and can be accessed by performing the following steps:

1. From within the vSphere Client, select **vCenter Server Settings** from the **Administration** drop-down menu.

2. Select **Advanced Settings** from the list box on the left-hand side of the window.

3. Add the appropriate key (see the following screenshot) and its associated value (true/false).

The following screenshot shows an example of disabling the RDM Filter:

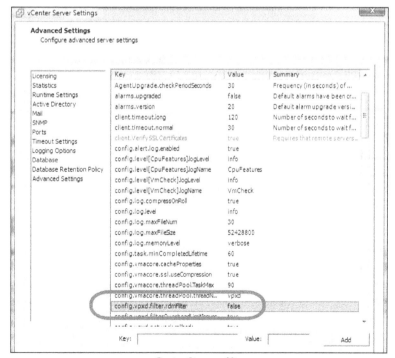

vCenter Storage filters

By default, all of the vCenter Storage filters are not shown in the **Advanced Settings** window of vCenter Server, but they are all functioning and have the value `true`, which means they are all enabled. They just will not show up inside the **Advanced Settings** window until we explicitly add them with a key/value pair.

Similar to claim rules, vCenter Server Storage filters are configuration options that we often overlook or forget about when troubleshooting storage visibility. If you make a change to an advanced setting, it's always a good idea to document the change, why it was made, and what the settings were originally. Otherwise, if it is an environment that you are not familiar with, it is invaluable to explore the vCenter Storage filter settings to ensure you have a strong understanding of why certain datastores are not available.

Disk resignaturing

When we mount or present a VMFS datastore to an ESXi host, we most commonly generate a new signature for that datastore. A signature is composed of many things, but the most important thing is the UUID that is generated inside the header of the datastore. This UUID provides the ESXi host with the ability to determine that each and every datastore is unique.

Most importantly, a virtual disk configuration from our VM guests point to this UUID in order to ensure compliance and security around the fact that the disks sit on a certain datastore. A key thing to remember with disk resignaturing and UUIDs is that we never want to have two datastores mounted with the exact same UUID at the same time. If this happens, ESXi is unable to determine where to send its SCSI commands and would begin to randomly transmit reads and writes to both datastores.

In most cases when adding a datastore, we will always want to generate a new UUID or signature. This is the default action suggested by vSphere when dealing with a duplicate UUID and datastore mount; however, there are some niche cases, mostly revolving around SAN snapshots and replication, where we will not want to generate a new UUID or resignature the datastore, but keep the original UUID.

For example, if one of our datastores was to become corrupt, we may want to present and mount a SAN snapshot that had been taken moments before the corruption occurred. When doing this, we would probably choose not to resignature the LUN and mount the datastore with the same UUID as it was before (SAN snapshots contain the same UUID as the LUN on which the snapshot was performed, since they are a block-by-block copy). By keeping the existing UUID, we save ourselves a bit of time in terms of virtual machine management.

VMs store information on the datastore where their virtual disks reside and use the datastore UUID to do so inside their configuration files. If a new UUID is generated, each VM configuration file must be updated, which is a tedious process if done manually. Alternatively, if we retain the existing signature, we could simply re-add all VMs to the inventory. Either option would take quite a bit of time which does not come without a price in an enterprise environment; however, the second option could be easily scripted.

 Only mount a datastore without resignaturing when you are absolutely sure that the original datastore will not come back online within vSphere. We never want to have two datastores with the same signature mounted to a host.

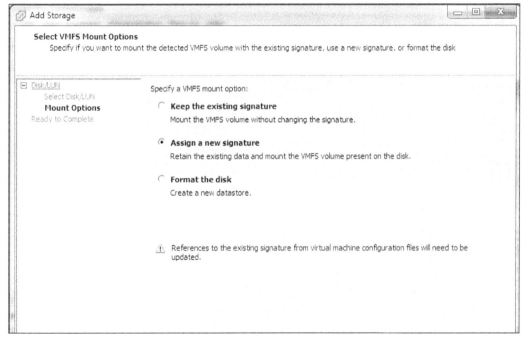

Options when adding a SAN snapshot

Following the same example of recovering from a SAN snapshot, the preceding screenshot shows us an example of the dialog box that is presented when we attempt to mount a datastore that doesn't contain a unique signature. We can see that we have three options on how to handle the addition of the datastore; keep existing signature, generate a new signature, or simply format the volume as a new VMFS datastore. In our example, since we are sure that the original datastore will never be remounted to our hosts, we can safely choose **Keep the existing signature**.

Prior to vSphere 4, all resignature options had to be performed from within the command-line interface and we can still do this today. In fact, as the case is with most CLI commands, we can actually see a bit more information about the LUN or snapshot we are trying to mount. By executing `esxcli storage vmfs snapshot list`, we are able to get information similar to that which is displayed in the following screenshot:

```
/var/log # esxcli storage vmfs snapshot list
52276696-e5085650-d1da-001e0bed96a2
   Volume Name: iSCSI-REP
   VMFS UUID: 52276696-e5085650-d1da-001e0bed96a2
   Can mount: true
   Reason for un-mountability:
   Can resignature: true
   Reason for non-resignaturability:
   Unresolved Extent Count: 1
/var/log #
```

Snapshot information from CLI

Using this command, we have the ability to view the UUID of the snapshot as well as any mounting or signature conflicts that may be present.

> For more information, you can view VMware's KB article dealing with signature conflicts located at `http://kb.vmware.com/selfservice/microsites/search.do?language=en_US&cmd=displayKC&externalId=1011387`.

Understanding a LUN's signature and how vSphere reacts in situations with duplicate UUIDs is a key step in troubleshooting vSphere Storage in a disaster recovery or critical data loss event where we are mounting and unmounting SAN snapshots.

LUN numbering

In addition to the identifiers that we talked about in *Chapter 1, Understanding vSphere Storage Concepts and Methodologies*, each and every LUN that is attached to an ESXi host also has a LUN ID. A LUN ID is a simple integer that the storage array assigns to each and every LUN that it hosts. ESXi is able to handle a maximum of 256 LUNs per host, and when we perform storage rescans, it starts with a LUN ID of 0 and ends with a LUN ID of 255. This is important because a LUN ID above 255 (that is 268) will never be discovered by the host as it stops scanning at 255.

> While it is not required, it is the best practice to use the same LUN ID for each host in your cluster.

The maximum LUN ID used in a storage rescan is configurable by an advanced setting within ESXi called **Disk.MaxLun**. This setting is located in the **Advanced Settings** section of a host's **Configuration** tab and must be set on a per-host basis. While lowering the default value can increase the speed of rescans and boot up, there is a risk that an administrator will provision a LUN with an ID greater than what they have set in **Disk.MaxLun**. ESXi will never see or discover that LUN. This will occur even if you are under the configuration maximum of 256 LUNs per host. If we experience issues with discovering block storage and can't access the LUN initially, **Disk.MaxLun** is a great setting to check.

Troubleshooting Fibre Channel storage visibility

Fibre Channel has been around since 1994 and is probably one of the most widely used and most reliable storage transports available today. Fibre Channel is deployed in a shared storage scenario utilizing Fibre Channel switches to interconnect the storage array and our vSphere hosts. This allows for multiple physical paths between our storage systems and VM hosts.

> Fibre Channel connectivity issues are often a result of latency which will be discussed in *Chapter 4, Troubleshooting Storage Contention*; however, visibility and connection issues may stem from within our storage switch fabric as well.

Fibre Channel zoning is the process of partitioning a Fibre Channel fabric into smaller chunks to restrict connectivity, visibility, and add a level of security to your Fibre Channel network. Zoning in the Fibre Channel fabric is similar to a firewall except allowing selective presentation between hosts and the storage array. We would not want to allow non-vSphere servers to access our VMFS storage, so using zoning for security prevents this unauthorized access. Zoning is performed at the switch level and can be applied in a couple of different scenarios. We can zone the ports, which basically authorizes one switch port to see another switch port. This is otherwise known as hard zoning. This means that if the device connected to the port moves, it will no longer have access. However, if a new device is connected to the zoned port, it will have access.

Another type of zoning is called **World Wide Name** (**WWN**) zoning, often referred to as soft zoning. WWN zoning is essentially the same as port-based zoning just replacing the ports with WWNs. This allows us to maintain access to the zone as devices are moved around on the switch as the WWN always stays with the device. Also, if a new device is plugged into a port where a WWN zone once existed, it will not automatically gain access.

Since zoning may be handled differently depending on your switch vendor, it is challenging to come up with a generic solution when troubleshooting storage visibility. Always follow your vendor recommendations for zoning configuration and always remember zoning when investigating Fibre Channel connectivity and visibility issues.

Registered State Change Notification (RSCN)

Whenever a change occurs inside a zone configuration, such as the addition or removal of new zones or the application of a completely new zone configuration, most Fibre Channel switches will issue an RSCN. An RSCN is a notification of any major changes to the zone configuration that is issued to all the nodes that are subscribed to receive them. By default, the drivers for the HBAs inside ESXi automatically subscribe to receive RSCNs. There are some cases where Fibre Channel switches and arrays may have RSCNs disabled, and in this case, the vSphere hosts will be unaware of any zone configuration changes.

Although suppressed RSCNs are not very common, they most certainly can affect storage visibility. If a zone configuration is modified to allow additional hosts to access the storage array without RSCNs, the host would have no idea about the array and the array would have no idea about the host. RSCNs allow the SCSI communication to occur between the host and the array immediately, in turn allowing the host to begin scanning for new LUNs on the array. Again, this is not a very common scenario; however, RSCN's is definitely something we should keep in the back of our minds when dealing with storage visibility.

Identifying and interpreting Fibre Channel connection issues in the logs

Nearly all of our Fibre Channel (along with many other transports) errors are logged inside ESXi. There is a significant amount of detail logged inside /var/log and honestly we would never be able to make sense of each and every log entry. As an initial step in troubleshooting, we often find that our Fibre Channel logs will reference SCSI somewhere within their log entry. The following command will display all log entries containing SCSI in the /var/log/ folder:

```
grep -r SCSI /var/log/* | less
```

Most of the log entries dealing with SCSI will return a SCSI sense code. More information on interpreting and decoding these codes in order to get to the root cause of a problem is explained in KB article 289902 located at `http://kb.vmware.com/selfservice/microsites/search.do?language=en_US&cmd=displayKC&externalId=289902`.

There are also a few advanced settings which can be changed to control the content of the issues being logged. These are configured as advanced settings in the hosts **Configuration** tab. SCSI log advanced settings are explained in the following table:

Setting	Default	Description
Scsi.LogCmdErrors	1	Logs SCSI device command errors
Scsi.LogMPCmdErrors	1	Logs SCSI Multipathing Plugin command errors
Scsi.LogScsiAborts	0	Logs aborts (successful and unsuccessful) on SCSI devices

Keep in mind that these are advanced settings and should always be accompanied by some documentation if we are to change them, such as what the default values were, what we changed them to, why, and when.

Troubleshooting IP storage visibility

Although most of the troubleshooting techniques between Fibre Channel and IP storage overlap (mostly between FC and iSCSI since they both use block transport and VMFS partition), there are quite a few differences between the two storage types. Since we are now using network adapters inside our hosts and network switches (as opposed to HBAs and FC switches), most of the same concepts around network security such as firewalls, routes, and so on will also be applied to our iSCSI and NFS storage.

Verifying network connectivity to our iSCSI and NFS array

The first step we should always take when experiencing connectivity issues to our network storage is to verify connectivity between our two endpoints; the host and the storage. This may include properly assigning network information to our hardware iSCSI initiators or properly creating a VMkernel port group for the software iSCSI initiator or NFS client. No matter what the issue is, we need to ensure that the connectivity to our arrays is available. This can be done using a simple ping command, however with ESX, the ping command would only exit through the service console.

Best practices often state that we should have a separate network for storage, or at the very least a separate VLAN, as well as a dedicated VMkernel interface to ensure our traffic is segregated. In order for a ping to exit through a VMkernel interface, we need to use a slightly modified VMware command called vmkping as shown in the following screenshot:

```
/var/log # vmkping 192.168.6.79
PING 192.168.6.79 (192.168.6.79): 56 data bytes

--- 192.168.6.79 ping statistics ---
3 packets transmitted, 0 packets received, 100% packet loss
/var/log #
```

vmkping without a response

 Differentiating between ping and vmkping is only relevant when using ESX. ESXi still contains both commands but ping is just a simple symbolic link to vmkping. Thus, ESXi always processes ping and vmkping as a vmkping command.

If we aren't receiving a response from vmkping (shown in the preceding screenshot), then we will have to dig a little deeper. Most commonly, this is a result of not having the correct network information such as IP address, subnet mask, and so on applied to either our hardware initiators or VMkernel ports. This should be the first thing that we check. Another possibility though could be an issue with static routes set up on the ESXi host itself. In order to view our routing tables on our hosts, we can use the following command:

esxcfg-route -l

Always check to see if there is a route set up on your host that could be causing your iSCSI or NFS traffic to be routed through the wrong gateway or the wrong network altogether. In some cases, there may have been multiple administrators in the environment or the network may have changed which causes routes set up on ESXi to be obsolete resulting in connectivity issues to your network storage device. If we need to remove any routes, we can do so by running the following command:

```
esxcfg-route -d <NETWORK> <GATEWAY>
```

For example, if we wanted to remove the route that sent traffic from `192.168.6.0/24` to a gateway with address `192.168.6.5`, we would enter `esxcfg-route -d 192.168.6.0/24 192.168.6.5`. And to re-add the correct route (if needed), we can use the following command:

```
esxcfg-route -a <NETWORK> <GATEWAY>
```

In this example, the proper gateway for my `192.168.6.0` network is `192.168.6.1`, so I would use the command `esxcfg-route -a 192.168.6.0/24 192.168.6.1` The following screenshot shows a successful execution of `vmkping` after configuring the proper routes in ESXi:

```
/var/log # vmkping 192.168.6.75
PING 192.168.6.75 (192.168.6.75): 56 data bytes
64 bytes from 192.168.6.75: icmp_seq=0 ttl=64 time=0.387 ms
64 bytes from 192.168.6.75: icmp_seq=1 ttl=64 time=0.289 ms
64 bytes from 192.168.6.75: icmp_seq=2 ttl=64 time=0.421 ms

--- 192.168.6.75 ping statistics ---
3 packets transmitted, 3 packets received, 0% packet loss
round-trip min/avg/max = 0.289/0.366/0.421 ms
/var/log #
```

A successful vmkping

Once we have verified network connectivity to our storage array, the next logical step to take if we are still experiencing connectivity issues is the port requirements of both iSCSI and NFS.

iSCSI and NFS port requirements

Since we are accessing our IP storage through our Ethernet network, the same fundamentals for troubleshooting networking can be applied when troubleshooting IP storage. We must ensure that the required ports are open not only on the hosts and storage arrays themselves, but also on any firewalls, proxies, or network devices that sit in between the hosts and their storage. The following table shows the required ports that are needed for iSCSI and NFS:

Port	Protocol	Source	Target	Description
111	TCP	ESX(i) host	NFS server	NFS Client – RPC Portmapper
111	UDP	ESX(i) host	NFS server	NFS Client – RPC Portmapper
2049	TCP	ESXi host (5.1.x)	NFS server	Transactions from NFS storage devices
2049	UDP	ESXi host (5.1.x)	NFS server	Transactions from NFS storage devices
3260	TCP	ESXi	iSCSI server	Transactions to iSCSI storage devices

Since there are a wide variety of firewalls in the market today, it is not possible for us to explain how to create rules for all of them. The key with this step is that we need to work with our firewall administrator to ensure that the ports in the preceding table are opened up. If you want to test whether you can connect to an IP address on a certain port from within the ESXi CLI, you can use the nc command. In the following example, we try and create a connection to 192.168.6.75 on port 3260 – the default iSCSI port. For NFS, we would replace this with 2049.

```
nc -z 192.168.6.75 3260
```

In addition to our network firewalls, ESXi contains its own built-in firewall. When you configure an iSCSI initiator on an ESXi host, the required local rules are enabled and opened up by default, allowing connections to any contactable IP on the network. NFS behaves a bit differently. When an NFS datastore is mounted to ESXi, the system first checks the status of the NFS client ruleset. If it is disabled, it is automatically enabled and the IP information of the NFS server is entered into the allowed IPs section of the rule. If the NFS client was already enabled, the allowed IPs section is simply updated with the NFS server IP if needed. Also, when NFS datastores are unmounted, those IP addresses are removed, and when there are no longer any NFS datastores existing on the host, the NFS client ruleset will be disabled.

If you find that you need to modify or enable these rules, you can do so manually through either the vSphere Client or the command-line interface. Just keep in mind that any information we modify will be persistent for any iSCSI modifications, but any NFS modifications will be overridden in the event we unmount all NFS datastores from the host, since the ruleset will be disabled.

The following are a few examples of some common CLI commands that we can execute to perform different functions on the ESXi firewall with regards to the iSCSI ruleset. These could easily be repeated for the NFS client ruleset by replacing `iSCSI` with `nfsClient`.

To list the status of our iSCSI ruleset, use the following command:

```
esxcli network firewall ruleset list | grep iSCSI
```

To enable or disable the iSCSI ruleset (choosing either true or false), use the following command:

```
esxcli network firewall ruleset -r iSCSI -e true/false
```

To further secure your iSCSI ruleset by only allowing connections to certain IP addresses, use the following command:

```
esxcli network firewall ruleset set -r iSCSI -a false
```

To list the allowed IP addresses, use the following command:

```
esxcli network firewall ruleset allowedip list -r iSCSI
```

To add an IP to the `allowedip` list, use the following command:

```
esxcli network firewall ruleset allowedip add -r iSCSI -i 192.168.6.75
```

To remove an IP from the `allowedip` list, use the following command:

```
esxcli network firewall ruleset allowedip remove -r iSCSI -i 192.16.6.75
```

All of this functionality is also available from within the vSphere Client if you are more comfortable with a GUI. It is highly encouraged that you become comfortable without the GUI as most troubleshooting tasks are done through command line and being able to quickly list and change rulesets using the CLI will save us valuable time during outages and issues.

CHAP authentication

Since iSCSI traverses an IP network to transfer its data, there isn't much security or protection around the packets containing the data being transported. To alleviate this, iSCSI has implemented CHAP, which basically authenticates initiators (located on host) to targets (located on arrays). CHAP can play a key role in vSphere Storage visibility. If we do not have it set up properly, no authentication will take place in turn resulting in no connection to our datastores.

ESXi supports a couple of different CHAP authentication methods depending on what type of initiator you are using. One-way CHAP (target authenticates initiator) is supported on all initiators, whereas mutual CHAP (bidirectional) is only available when using dependent hardware or the software initiator. The following table shows the different security models that vSphere supports when dealing with CHAP:

Security level	Description
Do not use CHAP	No CHAP authentication at all
Use one-way CHAP if required by target	The host will prefer not to use a CHAP connection, but if required by the target it will
Use one-way CHAP unless prohibited by target.	The host will prefer CHAP, but will accept non-CHAP connections from unsupported targets
Use one-way CHAP	The host will require a successful CHAP connection.
Use mutual CHAP	The host and target will require a successful CHAP connection

CHAP becomes very important when troubleshooting iSCSI storage visibility issues. If you have set your initiator to use CHAP and have either an incorrect or secret name, then your hosts may still see the desired LUN you wish to mount, but will never be able to access it.

CHAP authentication errors are not found within the GUI, which means you cannot see whether or not your visibility issues are due to CHAP while inside the vSphere Client. CHAP will log authentication messages to a few different places depending on the type of initiator you are using. For hardware iSCSI initiators, troubleshooting is mostly done through the initiator itself utilizing the BIOS and any other logging techniques implemented. For the software initiator, we are able to troubleshoot by looking through the ESXi logs. Since it's impossible to describe every hardware iSCSI initiator, we will focus mainly on the software initiator. In fact, I find that troubleshooting and debugging is easier to perform with the messages that the software initiator outputs so I will often enable it alongside a hardware initiator and duplicate the settings.

As mentioned previously, CHAP errors often fail silently within the GUI, but they are logged in `/var/log/syslog.log` and `/var/log/vobd.log` on the ESXi host. Following is an example of one of the messages that is displayed on a CHAP authentication failure:

```
2013-09-06T18:00:58Z iscsid: Login failed to authenticate with target
iqn.2011-03.org.example.istgt:target1
2013-09-06T18:00:58Z iscsid: Shutdown Session: iqn.2011-03.org.
example.istgt:target1 if=iscsi_vmk@vmk3 addr=192.168.6.75:3260 (TPGT:1
ISID:0x2)  (T1 C1) Reason=5
2013-09-06T18:00:58Z iscsid: Login Failed: iqn.2011-03.org.example.
istgt:target1 if=iscsi_vmk@vmk3 addr=192.168.6.75:3260 (TPGT:1
ISID:0x2) Reason: 00050201 (0x0201 Initiator could not be successfully
authenticated.)
```

Now it's pretty easy for us to look at the preceding logs and come to the conclusion that we are experiencing a CHAP authentication error; however, there are a few key pieces of information that are not very evident in these messages. First is the software iSCSI initiator error code. This is located in the logs directly after the `Reason:` text and are displayed either as a decimal number or two groups of four digits. Utilizing the information located in *Appendix C, iSCSI Error Codes*, under the *Interpreting software iSCSI error codes* section, we can come to the following conclusion; `Reason=5` in the second line indicates that there was a login failure and `Reason: 00050201` in the last line indicates that the initiator failed to log in to the target and the target has also indicated an authentication failure.

Certainly the above scenario could be resolved by double-checking our CHAP settings and secrets on both the initiator and the target. When utilizing CHAP and experiencing connection issues, we should always remember to check our logfiles for authentication related errors.

Identifying and interpreting iSCSI storage connection issues in the logs

You will find almost all of the iSCSI storage errors by browsing `/var/log/syslog.log` and looking for log entries that begin with `iscsid`. To list out all the current entries containing `iscsid` inside the whole log folder, you can run the following command:

```
grep -r iscsid /var/log/* | less
```

As stated in the CHAP section earlier, we can utilize the `Reason:` section of the log entry by breaking the eight digits into two groups of four and referencing the software iSCSI error codes in *Appendix C, iSCSI Error Codes*, to determine the actual errors that are causing these issues. For the most part, this will satisfy our troubleshooting needs but there may be times when we need even more information and this is where verbose logging comes into play.

Verbose iSCSI logging is enabled by setting the `option.loglevel` parameter to `999` inside an internal ESXi database. You can do this by executing the following command:

```
vmkiscsid -x "insert into internal (key,value) VALUES
  ('option.LogLevel','999');"
```

Remember that we should always disable verbose logging when we are finished with it. This is done by executing the following command:

```
vmkiscsid -x "delete from internal where key='option.LogLevel';"
```

Troubleshooting NFS storage

NFS shares some commonalities with iSCSI in the fact that it communicates with the storage array over the network; however fundamentally, the two storage transports are very different. iSCSI utilizes a block protocol whereas NFS provides vSphere with a version of file storage. ESXi uses Version 3 of NFS and does not contain a VMFS file system, which makes troubleshooting NFS storage much different than that of iSCSI. Thankfully, NFS is somewhat simplified and disassociated with ESXi, making it very easy to deploy and somewhat easier to troubleshoot.

To mount a NFS datastore in ESXi, you only need to provide the IP address or DNS name of your NFS server, the share name that you have setup for your mount point, and a datastore name.

> When mounting the same NFS datastore to multiple hosts, we should always ensure that we are using the same datastore name.

There are a limited number of things that can go wrong with NFS datastores in terms of visibility. Apart from following the steps outlined earlier in this chapter for verifying network connectivity to your array, most of the connection problems are due to ACLs and permissions.

NFS ACLs

We have seen how zoning and masking can help us restrict host access to Fibre Channel LUNs and how CHAP provides us a way to prevent our hosts from accessing our iSCSI LUNs. When implementing NFS, we control host access through an access control list (ACL). The NFS ACL determines which host can see which file export.

This is normally done by specifying an IP address, hostname, or network that can access the share. If we are receiving errors stating **The mount request was denied** when adding an NFS datastore, we should always confirm whether the NFS ACL lists on our storage array are present and configured properly.

NFS permissions

Most NFS servers have a set of permissions in which they can export the share to hosts. These normally include no access, read, read/write, and read/write allow root. In order for ESXi to properly host VMs on an NFS server, we need to have a minimum of read/write permissions. We should always ensure that we have the proper NFS security permissions applied to our datastores and that they are not mounted as read only unless that is our intention.

Identifying and interpreting NFS storage connection issues in the logs

Just as we have used logfiles to get more information and dig deeper into our iSCSI and Fibre Channel connection issues, we can do the same with NFS. NFS logs most of its entries to vmkernel.log, hostd.log, and vobd.log; so when searching for errors and issues, it's best to really just search through the complete /var/log folder with the following command:

```
grep -r nfs /var/log/* | less
```

In order to enable verbose NFS logging, we need to use the nfsstat3 service. To do this, we can use the following command:

```
esxcfg-advcfg -s 1 /NFS/LogNfsStat3
```

nfsstat3 will generate a huge amount of logging into your hostd logs with regards to how NFS is working and performing, so when we have completed our troubleshooting exercise, we must always set this value back to 0 by running the following:

```
esxcfg-advcfg -s 0 /NFS/LogNfsStat3
```

Summary

We should now have a solid understanding of how to troubleshoot issues dealing with connectivity to and visibility of vSphere Storage. We covered Fibre Channel, iSCSI, and NFS, the three most common storage transports utilized by vSphere. We went through some of the common and not-so-common issues that could affect visibility to our storage, such as vCenter Server storage filters, disk resignatures, CHAP authentication, and NFS ACLs, as well as how to identify and troubleshoot storage visibility issues using the logs that ESXi provides.

In the next chapter, we will go over how to spot and resolve issues we commonly see that relate to storage contention.

4
Troubleshooting Storage Contention

Now that we have learned about the various tools we can use to troubleshoot vSphere Storage and tackled the common issues that appear when we are trying to connect to our datastores, it's time for us to look at another type of issue with storage: contention. Storage contention is one of the most common causes of problems inside a virtual environment and is almost always the cause of slowness and performance issues.

One of the biggest benefits of virtualization is consolidation: the ability to take multiple workloads and run them on a smaller number of systems, clustered with shared resources, and with one management interface. That said, as soon as we begin to share these resources, contention is sure to occur. This chapter will help with some of the common issues we face pertaining to storage contention and performance.

This chapter will cover the following:

- Identifying storage contention and performance issues
- Planning—how to properly scale your storage
- vSphere features to help with latency, contention, placement, and compliance
- SCSI reservation conflicts
- Storage queuing in vSphere
- Troubleshooting NAS and iSCSI storage performance

Identifying storage contention and performance issues

One of the biggest causes of poor storage performance is quite often the result of high I/O latency values. Latency in its simplest definition is a measure of how long it takes for a single I/O request to occur from the standpoint of your virtualized applications. As we will find out later, vSphere further breaks the latency values down into more detailed and precise values based on individual components of the stack in order to aid us with troubleshooting.

But is storage latency always a bad thing? The answer to that is "it depends". Obviously, a high latency value is one of the least desirable metrics in terms of storage devices, but in terms of applications, it really depends on the type of workload we are running. Heavily utilized databases, for instance, are usually very sensitive when it comes to latency, often requiring very low latency values before exhibiting timeouts and degradation of performance.

There are however other applications, usually requiring throughput, which will not be as sensitive to latency and have a higher latency threshold. In all cases, we as vSphere administrators will always want to do our best to minimize storage latency and should be able to quickly identify issues related to latency.

As a vSphere administrator, we need to be able to monitor latency in our vSphere environment. This is where `esxtop` can be our number one tool. All of the storage related `esxtop` counters are fully explained in *Appendix B*, *Statistics of esxtop*, but for the sake of this chapter we will focus on three counters: `DAVG/cmd`, `KAVG/cmd`, and `GAVG/cmd`, all of which are explained in the following table:

Metric	Description	Threshold
`DAVG/cmd`	This is the average response time in milliseconds per command being sent from the VMkernel to the device.	25
`KAVG/cmd`	This is the amount of time in milliseconds the command spends inside VMkernel.	1-2
`GAVG/cmd`	This is the response time in milliseconds as the guest operating system perceives. Usually GAVG = KAVG + DAVG.	25

Storage columns in esxtop

> When looking at the thresholds outlined in the preceding table, we have to understand that these are developed as more of a recommendation rather than a hard rule. Certainly, 25 ms of device latency isn't good, but it will affect our applications in different ways, sometimes bad, sometimes not at all.

In *Chapter 2, Commonly Used Tools for Troubleshooting Storage*, we discussed how to use `esxtop` and how to switch between the various displays it offers. The following sections will outline how we can view latency statistics as they pertain to disk adapters, disk devices, and virtual machines.

Disk adapter latency statistics

By activating the disk adapter display in `esxtop`, we are able to view our latency statistics as they relate to our HBAs and paths. This is helpful in terms of troubleshooting as it allows us to determine if the issue resides only on a single HBA or a single path to our storage array, as shown in the following screenshot:

```
3:28:01pm up 38 days 21:11, 370 worlds, 8 VMs, 9 vCPUs; CPU load a
55, 0.52

ADAPTR PATH                  DAVG/cmd KAVG/cmd GAVG/cmd QAVG/cmd
vmhba0  -                        3.85     0.01     3.86     0.00
vmhba1  vmhba1:C0:T0:L0          0.00     0.00     0.00     0.00
vmhba1  vmhba1:C0:T0:L1          0.48     0.00     0.49     0.00
vmhba1  vmhba1:C0:T1:L0          0.00     0.00     0.00     0.00
vmhba1  vmhba1:C0:T1:L1          0.00     0.00     0.00     0.00
vmhba1  vmhba1:C0:T2:L0          0.00     0.00     0.00     0.00
vmhba1  vmhba1:C0:T2:L1          0.00     0.00     0.00     0.00
vmhba1  vmhba1:C0:T3:L0          0.00     0.00     0.00     0.00
vmhba1  vmhba1:C0:T3:L1          1.22     0.00     1.22     0.00
vmhba1  vmhba1:C0:T4:L0          0.00     0.00     0.00     0.00
vmhba2  vmhba2:C0:T0:L0          0.00     0.00     0.00     0.00
vmhba2  vmhba2:C0:T0:L1          0.68     0.00     0.69     0.00
vmhba2  vmhba2:C0:T1:L0          0.00     0.00     0.00     0.00
vmhba2  vmhba2:C0:T1:L1          0.00     0.00     0.00     0.00
vmhba2  vmhba2:C0:T2:L0          0.00     0.00     0.00     0.00
vmhba2  vmhba2:C0:T2:L1          0.00     0.00     0.00     0.00
vmhba2  vmhba2:C0:T3:L0          0.00     0.00     0.00     0.00
vmhba2  vmhba2:C0:T3:L1          0.63     0.00     0.64     0.00
vmhba2  vmhba2:C0:T4:L0          0.00     0.00     0.00     0.00
vmhba32 -                        0.00     0.00     0.00     0.00
```

Disk adapter latency statistics in esxtop

Use the following steps to activate the disk adapter latency display:

1. Start esxtop by executing the `esxtop` command.

2. Press *d* to switch to the disk adapter display.

3. Press *f* to select which columns you would like to display.

4. Toggle the fields by pressing their corresponding letters. In order to view latency statistics effectively, we need to ensure that we have turned on Adapter Name (*A*), Path Name (*B*), and Overall Latency Stats (*G*) at the very least.

5. If it is preferred, you can get a more detailed listing of the paths associated with an HBA by pressing *e* and entering in the associated adapter name.

> `esxtop` counters are also available for read and write latency specifically along with the overall latency statistics. This can be useful when troubleshooting storage latency as you may be experiencing quite a bit more write latency than read latency which can help you isolate the problems to different storage components. See *Appendix B, Statistics of esxtop*, for a complete list of storage related esxtop counters.

Disk device latency statistics

The disk device display is crucial when troubleshooting storage contention and latency issues as it allows us to segregate any issues that may be occurring on a LUN by LUN basis.

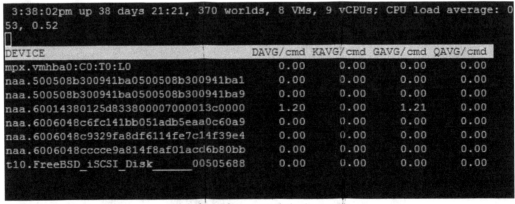

Disk device latency statistics in esxtop

Use the following steps to activate the disk device latency display:

1. Start esxtop by executing the `esxtop` command.
2. Press *u* to switch to the disk device display.
3. Press *f* to select which columns you would like to display.
4. Toggle the fields by pressing their corresponding letters. In order to view latency statistics effectively, we need to ensure that we have turned on Device Name (*A*) and Overall Latency Stats (*I*) at the very least.

> By default, the `Device` column is not long enough to display the full ID of each device. For troubleshooting, we will need the complete device ID. We can enlarge this column by pressing *L* and entering the length as an integer that we want.

Virtual machine latency statistics

The latency statistics displayed inside the virtual machine display are not displayed using the same column headers as the previous two views. Instead, they are displayed as `LAT/rd` and `LAT/wr`. These counters are measured in milliseconds and represent the amount of time it takes to issue an I/O request from the virtual machine. This is a great view that can be used to determine a couple of things. One, is it just one virtual machine that is experiencing latency? And two, is the latency observed on mostly reads or writes?

```
6:24:27pm up 39 days 8 min, 369 worlds, 8 VMs

VMNAME           LAT/rd LAT/wr
FreeNAS            0.00   0.00
vCenter            0.18   1.40
Debian-02          0.00   0.00
Debian-05          0.00   0.00
Debian-08          0.00   0.00
WinXP-01           0.00   0.00
Debian-09          0.00   0.00
WinXP-02           0.00   0.00
```

Virtual machine latency statistics in esxtop

Use the following steps to activate the virtual machine latency display:

1. Start esxtop by executing the `esxtop` command.

2. Press *v* to switch to the virtual machine disk display.

3. Press *f* to select which columns you would like to display.

4. Toggle the fields by pressing their corresponding letters. In order to view latency statistics effectively, we need to ensure that we have turned on VM Name (*B*), Read Latency Stats (*G*), and Write Latency Stats (*H*).

Using vCenter alarms to monitor latency

Viewing the latency statistics inside `esxtop` is crucial when troubleshooting storage performance related issues. The data in esxtop is real-time data though and we can't sit on esxtop all day long looking for spikes in latency. Thankfully, vCenter gives us the ability to create an alarm as it pertains to virtual machine latency using the **VM Max Total Disk Latency** trigger. Steps to set up the alarm are as follows:

1. Click your desired VM or parent object to create the alarm on and select the **Alarms** tab.

2. Click on the **Definitions** view and right-click anywhere within the blank space and select **New Alarm**.

3. Set the **Alarm Type Monitor** field to **Virtual Machine**.

4. Select the option **Monitor for specific conditions or state, for example, CPU usage, power state**.

5. On the **Triggers** tab, click on **Add**.

6. From the drop-down menu, select **VM Max Total Disk Latency**.

7. Here you can modify the warning and alert thresholds along with the condition length.

8. If you wish to add any alerting functionality such as e-mails or SNMP traps, you can do so in the **Actions** tab. When done click on **OK**.

VM Max Total Disk Latency trigger

Now that we have determined how to identify and monitor storage latency in vSphere, it's time to move on to how to resolve contention issues. The rest of this chapter will focus first on how to properly design your storage and then move on to how to resolve some common problems that cause our latency counters to rise.

With the release of vSphere 5.1, VMware has integrated certain portions of vCenter Operations. The vCenter Operations Management Suite can be a great tool to identify and troubleshoot storage issues in your environment. To learn more about vCenter Operations, visit the product page at `http://www.vmware.com/products/vcenter-operations-management`.

Planning – how to properly scale your storage

One of the best ways to avoid storage contention issues is to size your storage in terms of performance and throughput from the beginning. A properly sized and scalable storage array is the best foundation in terms of troubleshooting as it will go far in preventing most of the issues explained throughout this chapter. Unfortunately, it's not often that we get to start from a blank slate; however, if presented with the opportunity to deploy a new storage environment or migrate from an older array, we should use the tools and knowledge explained in this section to ensure that we match a suitable storage solution to that of our environment's workload and performance needs.

Traditionally, we measured storage performance by throughput, that is, how much data can we transfer within a given time frame. All too often, we also get caught in the trap of looking at raw capacity when making decisions around storage solutions. Using capacity and throughput as our main drivers in designing storage may have worked in the past, but in a shared-storage environment where we have multiple hosts accessing the storage array concurrently, we really have to focus on another metric: **Input/Output Operations per second (IOPs)**. IOPs measure the number of operations that a storage system can perform in one second. These commands can be read/write requests as well as metadata updates. This is very important in a virtualized infrastructure as it's common to see multiple VMs sending many small reads and writes to your storage, each requiring 1 IOPs. We need to ensure that our storage array can provide the amount of IOPs that our workloads require.

Calculating IOPs requirements

When we get the chance to build and design a storage infrastructure, whether it is for a new environment or an upgrade environment, it certainly helps if we understand the amount of IOPs that our workloads require in order to purchase a proper storage array. It sounds simple but this is one of the most challenging tasks you can undertake. There is a lot of published material based around some of the more popular applications such as Microsoft Exchange that will provide us with an average IOPs requirement based on the amount and types of users; however, capturing data from the actual workload and running in our environment utilizing tools such as PerfMon or vscsiStats will provide a more detailed and accurate representation of the amount of IOPs we will require.

You can view the current number of IOPs each VM is sending by monitoring the CMD/s column in esxtop. This, however, doesn't take into account the size of the I/O operation; to get a more detailed look at your application's IOPs, you are better off to use the tools such as Iometer and vscsiStats.

Calculating the number of disks required

Once we have the total number of IOPs required, we can begin to size up a storage solution. The first thing we should look at is the type or speed of the drives that will be in our array. The following table displays some of the common drive types and speeds along with the average number of IOPs they can perform. Now these numbers aren't set in stone, but are just the average industry baselines developed to aide us in our calculations.

Drive speed	Average IOPs
7200 RPM (SATA)	75
10K RPM (SAS)	125
15K RPM (SAS)	175
SSD	6000

Average IOPs for different drive speeds

So let's say that after our IOPs assessment, we determined that we required an array that could provide us with 17500 IOPs. You might think that's easy; just get 100 x 15K RPM SAS drives to satisfy the requirement (100 drives x 175 IOPs/drive). This would be true if we were to place these drives in a RAID 0 configuration, but a more likely situation will have us placing a RAID 1, 5, or 6 on the array. When we do this, we introduce what is called a RAID penalty. Take for instance RAID 5. When we issue one single write I/O to a group of drives in a RAID 5 array, due to parity and spanning, the array actually incurs four writes or four IOPs. RAID 6 provides us with an even higher write penalty since it calculates parity twice. The following table outlines some of the most common RAID write penalties.

Since we can use any disk for a read operation, no read penalties are incurred in the different RAID levels.

Raid level	Write penalty
RAID 0	1
RAID 1	2
RAID 5	4
RAID 6	6

Write penalties on RAID levels

So now that we are aware of the penalties in terms of write operations to our array, we can come to the conclusion that we will always require more disks to satisfy our IOPs when introducing RAID. To figure out the number of disks required, we can use the following formula. Keep in mind I'm assuming that our environment is split 50/50 in terms of reads and writes. This is the information that we would need to gather beforehand to properly design the solution as it can greatly affect the outcome of the formula.

$$\# disks = Req.IOPs * (\frac{Drive\ IOPs * Write\ \%}{RAID\ Penalty} + (Drive\ IOPs * Read\ \%))$$

So let's stick with our preceding example of setting 17500 as the required IOPs in our environment, 50% read, 50% write, 15K SAS drives in a RAID 5 configuration. When plugging the information into the formula, we will end up with the following formula:

$$\# disks = 17500 * (\frac{175 * .5}{4} + (175 * .5))$$

After doing the math, we can conclude that in order to satisfy our 17,500 IOPs in a RAID 5 configuration, we will need exactly 160 disks, 60 more than our initial assumption without RAID penalties. Also, in order to satisfy a variety of workload types, we are most likely going to have a mixture of RAID levels set up within our LUNs, forcing us to perform these calculations on a per-LUN basis which will further increase the number of disks we require.

This is just a very simplified version of how you can estimate the required number of disks you will need by calculating your functional IOPs. This can be one of the most challenging tasks we can face as a vSphere administrator; mainly due to the fact that each and every workload is unique. That said, proper storage planning, design, and implementation upfront will ensure better performance and reliability down the road so it's good to have a general understanding of how to calculate IOPs and design storage.

How do we know when we need more IOPs?

Since we don't get the luxury of designing a new storage solution for our environment every day, it's crucial that we properly monitor our current storage solution in terms of IOPs issued and IOPs aborted to determine when we might need to tweak it by adding more spindles or changing RAID configurations. Once again, esxtop will become our number one troubleshooting tool in this regard.

The most important metrics to monitor with regards to IOPs are **CMDS/S (Commands per second)** and **ABRTS/s (Aborts per second)**. In *Appendix B*, *Statistics of esxtop*, we can see that CMDS/s will be very close to the number of IOPs being issued, depending on the amount of metadata updates taking place and ABRTS/s is the number of times in one second that a command has been aborted by the guest OS. If the value inside the ABRTS/s column is anything other than zero, then we probably have some sort of storage contention issue, which means that the storage array is not processing the command in the specified amount of time that the OS requires.

> ABRTS/s does not always indicate that you require more IOPs. ABRTS/s can be caused by a number of things such as path saturation, array hardware issues, array caching issues, and so on. Another reason is it's important to understand our current environment's workload and IOP requirements.

You can enable the ABRTS/s column in esxtop on the disk adapter and disk device displays by activating the ERRSTAT statistics from the field selection. We can also view aborted commands on a per-VM basis by utilizing the performance graphs in vSphere Client and selecting the **Commands Aborted** metric.

IOPs are critical when it comes to vSphere Storage performance and lack of IOPs is often a cause of storage latency and slowness. It certainly helps our troubleshooting skills by understanding how to properly design and implement storage; however in most cases, we don't have the luxury of completely overhauling our storage environments. In this case, we can use some built-in features that come with vSphere to help alleviate some of those management tasks revolving around LUN balancing, latency, and placement.

vSphere features to help with latency, contention, placement, and compliance

Sizing storage is normally done on a per-datastore basis which allows us to provide many different speeds and RAID levels to support different application requirements. For instance, it's not uncommon to have a RAID 10 LUN hosting a variety of database applications and a RAID 5 LUN hosting web servers. In the beginning, this is easy for us to manage; we simply place our VM on the proper datastore based on its needs and requirements. Despite our best initial design though, as we perform upgrades and configuration changes that could result in our VM running on the wrong datastore and not getting the performance that it requires, we commonly begin to experience slow performance and high latency. vSphere contains some native features that help us in terms of VM placement and compliance: **Storage DRS (SDRS)** and Profile-Driven Storage (both available only in Enterprise Plus licensing packages).

Profile-Driven Storage

Profile-Driven Storage is a feature of vSphere that allows the administrator to easily and automatically determine which datastore or datastore cluster can provide us with the performance and functionality requirements for a given VM. This is done by assigning either user-defined or vendor-defined storage capabilities to a datastore, grouping the individual capabilities into a profile, and assigning that profile to a VM. Now when we are deploying a new virtual machine, we can see our datastores broken into two categories: compatible and incompatible. These categories provide us with a way to determine whether our VMs are compliant in terms of getting the resources and performance they need out of their underlying datastore.

The first step of setting up Profile-Driven Storage is to assign storage capabilities to a datastore. Some arrays that support the **vSphere APIs for Storage Awareness (VASA)** feature are able to present storage capabilities directly to vSphere. For those that don't support VASA, we can manually configure these storage capabilities. For the sake of our example, we will be adding user-defined storage capabilities.

The following steps explain the process of adding a user-defined storage capability to a datastore:

1. Right-click on a datastore and select **Assign User-Defined Storage Capability**.

2. Select a previously created storage capability from the drop-down box or select **New** to create a new one.

3. Click on **OK** when finished.

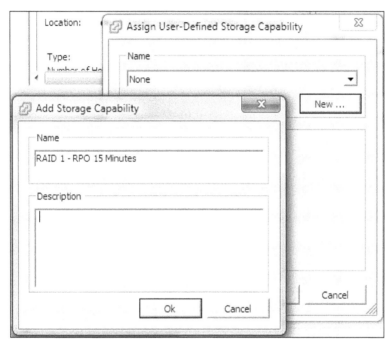

User-Defined Storage Capabilities

At this point, we need to create a storage profile containing our storage capability which will be assigned to a VM. To do so, we can use the following steps:

1. Select **VM Storage Profiles** from the home screen.

2. Click on the **Create VM Storage Profile** button.

3. Give our storage profile a name and description, and then click on **Next**.

4. Check the relevant storage capabilities for the profile, click on **Next,** and then click on **Finish**.

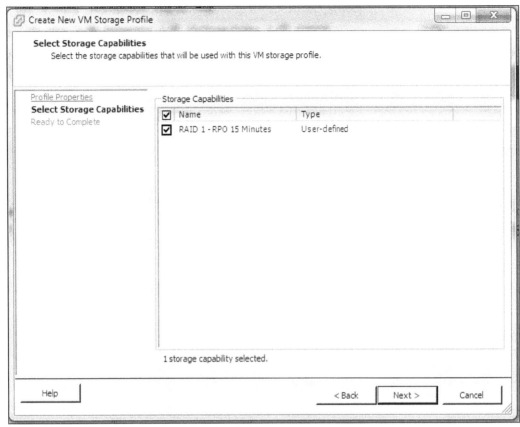

New VM storage profile

 Since we are able to assign only one user-defined storage capability to a datastore, it's best to include just one capability in each storage profile. If we were to assign more than one capability to the profile, we would never be able to bring VMs attached to that profile into compliance.

Finally, we are left with the task of assigning the profile to a VM. This is done using the following steps:

1. Right-click on the VM and select **Edit Settings**.
2. On the **Profiles** tab, select the desired profile from the **Storage Profile** drop-down box. We can also use this screen to apply separate profiles to individual disks within that VM if we wish.

We are now able to view virtual machine compliance in terms of storage profiles by looking at the VMs **Summary** page. This information can also be viewed per profile on the main storage profile page, stating whether a VM is compliant or not compliant.

Profile-Driven Storage gives us an easy way to determine if our VMs are sitting on the proper underlying storage. It makes troubleshooting much faster as we can quickly determine if a VM is out of compliance, which may be the reason why we are experiencing slowness or latency. There is, however, no automation in place with Profile-Driven Storage; thus it is simply a reporting tool at this point. If automation is what you are looking for, Storage DRS may be a better choice.

Storage DRS for performance

DRS allow us to utilize a pool of distributed CPU and memory resources ensuring that resources are distributed relatively across all the VMs. Storage DRS does much the same thing, however it also balances our storage space usage and storage I/O levels. SDRS is not a troubleshooting tool; it's more of a proactive feature that can help us prevent storage issues and contention from happening. SDRS does this by grouping two or more datastores that are similar in nature into a datastore cluster. When deploying a VM, we now specify which datastore cluster we would like to place the VM on rather than the individual datastore. SDRS can then calculate an optimal datastore to deploy the VM to, depending on capacity and latency metrics that it has collected over time.

In addition to placement, SDRS can also help us in terms of ongoing monitoring of latency for our VMs. Every eight hours, SDRS will run the VM latency statistics through its performance algorithms and determine which VMs qualify as candidates to Storage vMotion in order to meet a datastore's specific latency thresholds. In doing so, SDRS tries to maintain its latency threshold (default of 15 ms) on all other datastores within the datastore cluster. SDRS generates recommendations, and if set to the **Fully Automated** mode, it will apply those recommendations to the VMs. Otherwise, when set to the **No Automation (Manual mode)** mode, recommendations are just noted and can be applied manually if desired.

SDRS can also be enabled or disabled on a per-VM basis. In some cases, such as a database with a high workload, we may want to disable SDRS on that specific VM, yet have it monitor all other VMs. This can be configured through the **Virtual Machine Settings** section of a cluster's SRDS settings.

The default latency threshold of 15 ms is a recommendation from VMware. We do have the ability to change this, as this value could be high or low depending on the underlying storage we are using.

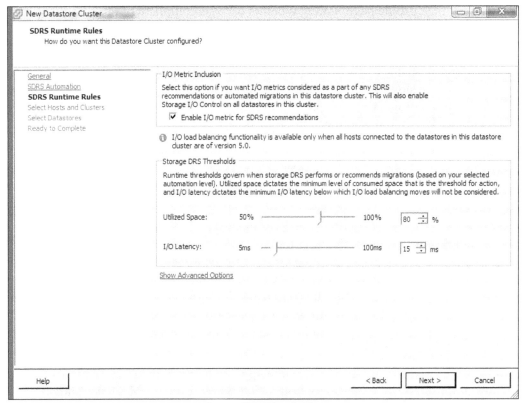

Storage DRS Thresholds

Enabling SDRS and creating a datastore cluster is a very simple process and can be carried out as follows:

1. In the **Datastores and Datastore Clusters** inventory view, right-click on a datacenter and select **New Datastore Cluster**.

2. Give your datastore cluster a name and then click on **Next**.

3. Set your desired automation level (**No Automation (Manual mode)** results in simple recommendations, **Fully Automated** applies the recommendations) and then click on **Next**.

4. Configure your thresholds (80% **Utilized Space** and 15 ms **I/O Latency**). You can also specify whether to use I/O metrics collected from **Storage I/O Control** (**SIOC**) to determine the latency values. If choosing this, Storage I/O Control will be enabled on all the datastores inside the datastore cluster.

5. Finish the wizard by adding the hosts and datastores that you wish to include into the cluster.

Keep in mind that there is plenty that goes on "under the hood" with SDRS when utilizing it for I/O balancing and it's usually best to just leave it alone and let it handle the recommendations. There is also a piece of software in SDRS which handles placement based on capacity and disk utilization which will be discussed more in *Chapter 5, Troubleshooting Storage Capacity and Overcommitment*.

Another important note is that SDRS is not a solution to undersized, over provisioned, or connection/latency issues and can actually impose risks on our environment if experiencing issues caused by other measures such as SCSI reservation conflicts. That said, SRDS applies the recommendations and performs Storage vMotion operations in the off hours when production workloads are not heavily utilized and is still a great solution to implement to balance out your workloads in terms of latency.

SCSI reservation conflicts

The benefits of having a shared storage alongside ESXi are no secret. It allows us to take advantage of a lot of vSphere features such as vMotion, HA, and DRS. However, with all these features and benefits come a few restrictions as well. Since we have multiple hosts with access to the same storage, ESXi needs to ensure that when one host is writing or modifying the metadata of a LUN, no other host is doing so at the same time in order to prevent data corruption or data loss.

The metadata on a VMFS datastore is essentially just mapping information which points to all the files, directories, pointers, and objects that reside on that datastore. When most virtual machine and datastore management functions are performed, this metadata requires an update. Below are some of the actions that will trigger a metadata update:

• Powering a virtual machine on or off

• Creating a new virtual machine or template

- Deploying a virtual machine from template
- Migrating a virtual machine to another host
- Creating, deleting, modifying or extending a datastore

As we can see, most of the operations that trigger metadata updates are quite common tasks and happen very often. When we trigger any of the preceding options, ESXi needs to implement a locking system on the datastore to ensure that no other hosts are writing to the datastore concurrently. The two locking mechanisms that ESXi supports are SCSI reservations and **Atomic Set & Test** (**ATS**).

SCSI reservations will lock an entire LUN while the management operations are being performed and subsequently unlock the LUN when they have completed. If your storage array is compatible with **vStorage APIs for Array Integration** (**VAAI**) or hardware acceleration, ESXi can utilize ATS in place of SCSI reservations.

ATS is essentially the same thing as SCSI reservations; however, instead of locking the entire LUN, the locks are done on a per-sector or per-block basis. This allows other operations targeting the metadata to continue, making it a much more preferable solution. However, we rely on storage hardware vendors to enable these features, which makes VAAI support limited, that is, there are times when we have no alternatives but to utilize SCSI reservations as our locking mechanism.

 Any VMFS5 datastore created on a VAAI capable array will use ATS only. In the case you need to disable ATS and revert to SCSI reservations, you can do so by disabling the **DataMover. HardwareAcceleratedLocking** setting located in the advanced settings of a host. Keep in mind your LUN must be offline in order to do this.

When a SCSI reservation is issued to a datastore by a host, no other hosts can perform management functions that require metadata updates on that datastore. When another host attempts to issue a reservation to an already reserved LUN, access is denied and a reservation conflict occurs. By default, the host experiencing the conflict will try and reestablish the lock after a 50 ms delay and will attempt this 80 times.

 The number of retry attempts can be modified with the **SCSI. ConflictRetries** advanced setting; however, if we need to modify this from the default of 80, we probably have bigger issues that need to be explored.

When an ESXi host issues many SCSI reservations, the chances of experiencing a SCSI reservation conflict from another hosts increases. When we begin to experience multiple reservation conflicts, latency increases, performance decreases, and applications and datastores can become unresponsive. This is why it is important that we understand how to monitor our system for SCSI reservation conflicts.

Monitoring SCSI reservation conflicts with esxtop

When SCSI reservation conflicts are occurring, ESXi will log numerous entries into the vmkernel.log file containing the phrase **reservation conflict**. By filtering through the logs, we can determine if reservation conflicts are occurring but we can't really pinpoint how many or how often without some sort of log analyzer.

Thankfully, esxtop has a couple of counters to help us examine SCSI reservations and reservation conflicts in real time; RESV/s (amount of SCSI reservations per second) and CONS/s (number of SCSI reservation conflicts per second).

```
6:27:50pm up 14 days  3:31, 390 worlds, 6 VMs, 7 vCPUs; CPU load average: 0.52, 0.48, 0.51

ADAPTR NPTH AQLEN   CMDS/s   READS/s WRITES/s MBREAD/s MBWRTN/s   RESV/s   CONS/s
vmhba0    1   128     0.00      0.00     0.00     0.00     0.00     0.00     0.00
vmhba1    9  2176     4.77      0.00     4.77     0.00     0.02     0.00     0.00
vmhba2    9  2176     0.00      0.00     0.00     0.00     0.00     0.00     0.00
vmhba32   6  1024     0.00      0.00     0.00     0.00     0.00     0.00     0.00
```

Monitoring SCSI reservations and conflicts within esxtop

Use the following steps to monitor SCSI Reservations within either the disk adapter or disk device display:

1. Start esxtop by executing the esxtop command.
2. Press *d* or *u* to switch to either the disk adapter or disk device display.
3. Press *f* to select which columns we would like to display.
4. Toggle the fields by pressing their corresponding letters. In order to view reservation conflicts effectively, we need to ensure that we have turned on the REVSTATS column (*F* inside disk adapter and *H* inside disk device).

For the most part, we can ignore the RESV/s column. A non-zero value in this column simply means that the host has issued a SCSI reservation due to the fact that it is performing a metadata update. This is normal activity. The CONS/s column however should be closely monitored. The CONS/s column will be populated when a host attempts to obtain a lock on a LUN through a SCSI reservation and the LUN has already been locked by another host. While there is no specific peak threshold, a good number to monitor for is 20 CONS/s which indicates that there are 20 active conflicts per second. Anything above this and it may result in some of the symptoms explained earlier (latency, unresponsive datastores and applications).

Resolving excessive SCSI resolutions

If we are consistently experiencing storage performance issues and we are seeing 20 or more SCSI reservations conflicts, then we should take action to reduce the number of SCSI reservation conflicts occurring. While this may not be the only issue, it may be a symptom of a larger issue and we need to eliminate this to get the source problem.

VMware has a great KB article outlining the steps we can take to troubleshoot and resolve SCSI reservation conflicts located at
http://kb.vmware.com/selfservice/microsites/search.
do?language=en_US&cmd=displayKC&externalId=1005009.

Since many of the resolutions differ depending on which storage array you are using, it's not relevant to explain them all here. Instead, we will outline a few of the common steps included in the KB article 1005009 that we can perform no matter which vendor's storage array we have implemented:

- If your array supports VAAI or hardware acceleration, use ATS.
    - ATS is the hardware accelerated replacement for SCSI reservations. As mentioned earlier, ATS will perform a block-level lock on specific metadata rather than locking a complete LUN. If it is possible to enable ATS or VAAI, use it.

- Serialize the operations of the shared LUNs; if possible, limit the number of operations on different hosts that require SCSI reservation at the same time

  ○ This basically means spreading the load across the LUNs and hosts. If we have a lot of VMs that are frequently being powered on or off on the same host, in turn, we will have a lot of SCSI reservations being issued to LUNs from that same host. Therefore, if we are able to spread these VMs that frequently perform functions that require SCSI reservations across other hosts in our cluster, we can limit the number of reservations being issued from one host, ultimately decreasing our chances of experiencing a SCSI reservation conflict.

- Increase the number of LUNs and limit the number of hosts accessing the same LUN.

  ○ By presenting more LUNs to store virtual machines into our cluster, we are able to decrease the amount of SCSI reservations being performed on one single LUN, thus limiting the number of times that LUN is locked for a metadata update.

- Reduce the number of snapshots. Snapshots cause numerous SCSI reservations.

  ○ When we operate using a vSphere snapshot, we are dynamically growing a delta file. Each time it needs to grow, we need to issue a SCSI reservation. It is ideal to keep the number of snapshots in your environment to a minimum as this is not the only operational performance challenge they present.

- Reduce the number of virtual machines per LUN. Follow recommendations in configuration maximums.

  ○ By limiting the number of VMs per LUN, we decrease the number of VM management functions being performed on that LUN. This, in turn, decreases the chance that multiple hosts will need to access the metadata on the LUN at the same time

If we are still experiencing issues after performing the above steps and other array-specific steps listed within the KB article 1005009, or if we simply are unable to view the LUN in question, then it is most likely that a host has issued a reservation on the LUN and has never released it. Unfortunately, there is no easy way to determine which host did it. At this point, we need to run the following command on each host in order to determine which host has issued the reservation:

```
esxcfg-info | grep -B16 -i "Pending Reservations"
```

For the most part, we should see that all of the LUNs have a value of 0 for "pending reservations"; however, sometimes we will see the output shown as follows where a LUN does in fact have a pending reservation:

```
|----Console Device................................ /vmfs/devices/
disks/naa.60014380125d833800007000013c0000
|----Devfs Path................................... /vmfs/devices/
disks/naa.60014380125d833800007000013c0000
|----Size........................................214748364800
|----Block Size..................................512
|----Number of Blocks............................419430400
|----SCSI Level..................................5
|----Queue Depth.................................128
|----Is Pseudo...................................false
|----Is Reserved.................................false
|----Is Perennially Reserved.....................false
|----Queue Full Sample Size......................0
|----Queue Full Threshold........................0
|----Is Offline..................................false
|----Is Local...................................false
|----Is SSD.....................................false
|----Is Thin Provisioned........................false
|----Pending Reservations.......................1
```

In such a case, we need to perform what is called a LUN reset to clear the lock on the LUN. The LUN reset needs to be executed from the host that is holding the reservation. Using the data displayed in the preceding example, in order to clear the lock, we would need to run the following command using the LUN's identifier:

```
vmkfstools -lock -lunreset
  /vmfs/devices/disks/naa.60014380125d833800007000013c0000
```

We can run the same `esxcfg-info` command again on the host ensuring that the LUN reset has been processed. If it has, the `Pending Reservations` field should return a value 0.

Generally, we can avoid SCSI reservation conflicts by simply changing our operational processes. These changes include changes such as serializing our operations that we perform, which means ensuring one process requiring a reservation has completed before kicking off another and by ensuring that we always perform our management operations through vCenter Server rather than on the vSphere host directly. vCenter is able to queue up the operations and manage the thresholds across the entire host cluster, which is one of key features of centralized management. Despite all of our best planning, issues will still pop up and having the fundamental knowledge on how to troubleshoot and isolate these issues is essential when troubleshooting vSphere Storage.

Storage queuing in vSphere

When I/O is issued from a virtual machine, it doesn't simply go straight to our storage. It actually passes through multiple queues from within the OS itself, the ESXi storage stack, the physical HBA, and also the storage array. In general, we can trust that the default values set up for the depth of these queues is sufficient for any environment. However there are situations, mainly dealing with older versions of vSphere and low VM densities, where adjusting queue depth values will benefit certain workloads. Making changes to the storage queues should not be a step taken lightly, and without properly understanding the way these queues function, we can actually cause a higher latency value by deviating from the defaults.

OS queue

The first queue that an I/O request will hit is the device driver queue of the VM's virtual SCSI adapter. The size of the driver queue will vary depending on the type of virtual SCSI adapter it is passing through. For the most part, we see this set at a default of 32 active commands that are being issued concurrently, with the exception of the PVSCSI adapter defaulting to 64. Once the I/O has passed through the OS queue it heads to the ESXi stack.

 The default values of these queues can be changed by modifying the Windows registry. See KB Article 1017423 located at http://kb.vmware.com/selfservice/ microsites/search.do?language=en_US&cmd=display KC&externalId=1017423 for more information.

Adapter queue

After the I/O has passed through the virtual machine, it is then placed into the queue of the physical HBA. The default value of this queue varies depending on the vendor and type of HBA; however, it is normally a higher number (1024+) and is applied on a per-port basis of the HBA. It's not often we experience issues where we would need to adjust the adapter queue depth.

Per-LUN queue

The per-LUN queue (sometimes referred to as the per-device queue) resides inside the HBA driver in the ESXi stack. The default value of this queue varies depending on the type of HBA present; however, the value is usually either 32 or 64. When this queue fills up, provided more than one VM is issuing traffic, vSphere will throttle this queue down to 32 in order to provide fairness to all of the VMs, as well as prevent one single VM from obtaining the complete queue while other VMs I/O requests sit and wait inside the VMkernel. The value of 32 comes from an advance setting in vSphere called **Disk.SchedNumReqOutstanding** which will be discussed a bit later in this section.

> **Disk.SchedNumReqOutstanding** will only be activated when I/O is detected from more than a single VM. If all the I/O is coming from a single VM, ESXi does not throttle down the per-LUN queue as there is no need to satisfy requests from other VMs, allowing the single VM to utilize the queue as needed.

Viewing queues in ESXi

Once again, our troubleshooting tool is going to be esxtop. As difficult and complex as the queuing mechanisms are for ESXi, it's actually quite easy to monitor and determine on a high level what his happening. When troubleshooting queuing in vSphere, we should pay attention to a few counters in esxtop, all listed within the following table and illustrated in the following figure:

Counter	Description
DQLEN	The per-LUN queue depth
ACTV	The number of active or in-flight commands currently being processed by the VMkernel
QUED	The number of commands which are waiting to be processed or inserted into the queue

Counter	Description
%USED	The percentage of queue depth used by active commands
LOAD	The ratio of the sum of VMkernel active commands and VMkernel queued commands to the queue depth

esxtop queue counters

Use the following steps to monitor queue statistics within the disk device display:

1. Start esxtop by executing the `esxtop` command.
2. Press *u* to switch to the disk device display.
3. Press *f* to select which columns you would like to display.
4. Toggle the fields by pressing their corresponding letters. In order to view queue statistics effectively, we need to ensure that we have turned on the `Queue Stats` column (*F*).

As we can see in the preceding screenshot, we are definitely experiencing some queuing issues on our iSCSI LUN. Any value other than 0 inside the `QUED` column indicates that we have exhausted our per-LUN queue and have commands waiting inside the VMkernel to be processed. We can also see the effects of this in terms of latency statistics (`DAVG`, `KAVG`, and `GAVG`) as their values have risen above the thresholds (discussed earlier in this chapter). Another notable observation we can make is that the LUN queue (normally 128) has switched to 32. This is the effect of the **Disk.SchedNumReqOutstanding** (DSNRO) advanced setting kicking in.

There is a lot of documentation that claims changing DSNRO to that of your per-LUN queue will help in terms of performance. In some cases, however, DSNRO along with a few other advanced settings helps in eliminating a "noisy neighbor" scenario where a single VM could obtain most of the storage resources. It also helps funnel the traffic to our storage arrays so as to not overload them or flood them with requests.

So when we look at the three types of queues, we can conclude that increasing the per-VM queue would not do much good as we could be throttled on down the line at the per-LUN queue. In this case, it seems to make sense to increase both the per-VM and per-LUN queues. However, if we change the value of the per-LUN queue, we increase the chances of saturating a single LUN and affecting other hosts within the cluster, eliminating the "fairness" that vSphere provides us with.

We have to be careful to assume the queue depth is a source issue. Quite often, we will find that the storage array cannot handle the workload that has been assigned to it, or may have an issue with configuration or the hardware which triggered the issue. It is important to ensure the array cache is configured correctly and that there are no failed components such as hard drives or controller components.

It is important that we approach queuing with caution and only look at changing these queue values when instructed to do so by VMware or our storage vendors. If we are looking to provide a more precise and safer way to provide throughput and IOPs on a per-VM basis across all of your hosts without touching queuing, we should consider implementing features such as Storage I/O Control.

vSphere Storage I/O Control

Storage I/O Control mimics the sharing mechanisms that resource pools provide, except instead of applying these shares on CPU or memory, SIOC applies them to disks within the virtual machines. SIOC shares are set up on a per-VM basis, whereas the contention thresholds are set up on the individual datastores. SIOC behaves a bit different than the DSNRO queuing mechanisms.

DSNRO will not adjust the per-LUN queue until a "queue full" condition has been met, whereas SIOC actively monitors our datastores for a congestion threshold (by default 30 ms). When that threshold is met, SIOC will dynamically implement a new per-LUN queue value per host, taking into consideration share values which are set up on our VMs as well as the **Max IOPS** setting that can also configured on a per-VM basis. By utilizing SIOC, we benefit by allocating each VM portions of the per-LUN queue; allowing certain guests more access to the queue than others and providing us with more granular control over the storage resources consumed by the VMs.

Configuring Storage I/O Control

VMware makes the task of enabling SIOC quite easy. To start, we need to enable Storage I/O Control on each and every datastore that we wish to apply the sharing mechanism to.

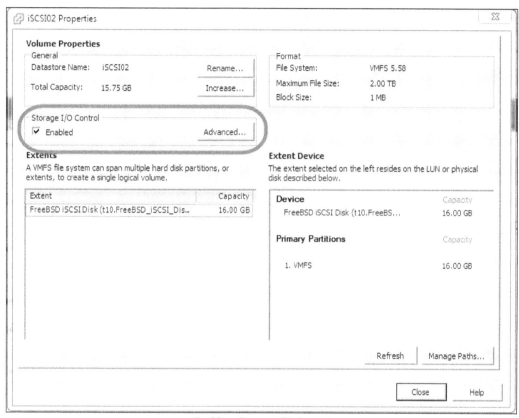

Enabling Storage I/O Control

To enable SIOC, use the following steps:

1. Enter the **Datastores and Datastore Clusters** inventory view.

2. Select the desired datastore, move to the **Configuration** tab, and then click on **Properties**.

3. Check the checkbox next to **Enabled** in the **Storage I/O Control** section. The **Advanced** button allows you to change the default congestion threshold.

Enabling SIOC is only half of the configuration we need to complete. We now need to assign shares to each of our VM's disks. We can think of SIOC disk shares in the same context as DRS memory and CPU shares. Each share value defined represents a relative portion of the total amount of shares. For instance, if we had VM A set up with 2000 shares and VM B setup with 1000, VM A would get twice the allocated queue spots (if required) than VM B.

The previous statement includes "if required" because SIOC will only apply shares and throttling in the event that we are experiencing contention on our storage.

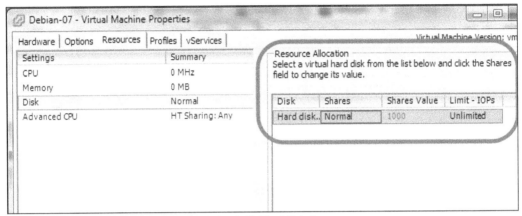

Assigning individual disk shares

To assign shares to a VMs virtual disk (VMDK), use the following steps:

1. Right-click on the desired VM and select **Edit Settings**.
2. Select **Disk** under the **Resources** tab.
3. Apply the desired share and IOPs limit to each virtual disk inside the VM.

As we can see, enabling and configuring Storage I/O Control is a lot easier and comes with a lower risk than monitoring and adjusting queues and queue depth manually. Unless otherwise requested by VMware support or our storage vendors, we should try to refrain from adjusting queue values. SIOC gives us an easy-to-use, efficient alternative of handling access to storage during peak times and can at most times be the answer to latency and slowness caused by storage queues.

Currently, SIOC is only available when utilizing vSphere Enterprise Plus licensing.

Troubleshooting NAS/iSCSI storage performance

When it comes to troubleshooting storage performance, most of the components, features, and issues that we have spoken about will apply to both Fibre Channel and network-driven storage. Apart from implementing faster networks such as upgrading from 1 GB to 10 GB, there are a few things that we can do that are specific to iSCSI and NFS inside vSphere to help us gain more performance from our network storage.

iSCSI port binding and Round Robin path policy

Although binding ports for the purpose of iSCSI storage will not improve throughput by itself, it does provide a stepping stone that allows us to enable the Round Robin path selection policy. By enabling Round Robin, we can evenly spread the load through multiple paths which can help to improve I/O performance of our iSCSI arrays.

iSCSI port binding is done differently than the standard NIC teaming functionality that is built into vSphere. According to best practices documents, it's not recommended at all to use any teaming policy on your NICs that are used for iSCSI connections. Port binding essentially takes two or more VMkernel ports which have been configured on the same network as your iSCSI array and binds them together. In the past, port binding could only be configured via CLI; however, since vSphere 5.0 we have the ability to do this inside vSphere Client. For the purposes of the following example, we will be using vSphere Client and the software iSCSI initiator.

The first step to setting up port binding is to configure a couple of VMkernel ports. This can be done in a variety of ways; however, the most important thing we need to remember is that each VMkernel port must transmit out of different physical NICs. In that sense, we could set up one vSwitch containing both VMkernel ports and then set our active and unused values on the physical NICs attached.

In the following figure, I have taken a different route of setting up two completely separate vSwitches, each containing a single VMkernel port and having only one physical NIC attached.

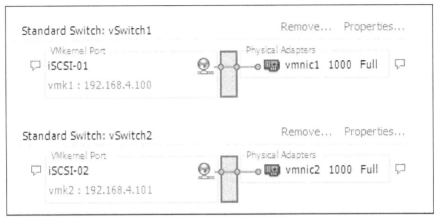

VMkernel port setup

Once we have the proper VMkernel ports configured, the next step is to bind these ports to our iSCSI initiator. This process is quite simple and is performed on the **Network Configuration** tab of our iSCSI initiators properties. The following figure shows our newly created VMkernel ports bound to our initiator:

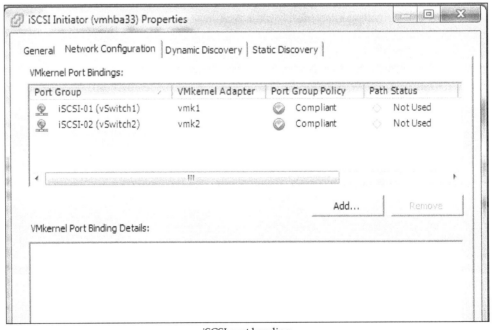

iSCSI port bonding

The following steps outline how to bind our two VMkernel ports to our iSCSI initiator:

1. Right-click on the iSCSI software initiator and select **Properties**.
2. From the **Network Configuration** tab, click on **Add**.
3. Select the VMkernel port you wish to use from the list and then click on **OK**.
4. Repeat the above step for all the VMkernel ports you wish to bind together.
5. When completed, click on **Close**.

In terms of port binding, we are now done. Our iSCSI initiator is now set up to use both VMkernel ports to transmit data to our iSCSI array. Multipathing and Round Robin, however, still need to be configured. This is done the same way as we described in *Chapter 3, Troubleshooting Storage Visibility*, and is performed on a per-LUN basis unless other rules have been defined.

 When using VMkernel port binding and iSCSI, we need be sure that any ACLs configured on our iSCSI array include the IP address of each VMkernel port we are using.

Although the intention of iSCSI port binding is to provide high availability rather than enhancing performance, we can utilize the Round Robin path policy to gain a little extra throughput to and from our iSCSI array. Even if you are not looking to get extra performance, I would always recommend that we use port binding in order to, at the very least, gain the HA and failover functionality that redundant NICs and paths provide.

Jumbo Frames and MTU size

Administrators will often increase the size of the MTU from 1500 to 9000 in order to support Jumbo Frames and ultimately provide some higher throughput to their iSCSI array. This is commonly done inside vSphere Client by modifying the MTU size on the VMkernel port associated with the iSCSI network, but can also be set via the command line utilizing the following command.

To increase the MTU on a vSwitch, use the following command:

```
esxcli network vswitch standard set -m 9000 -v vSwitch#
```

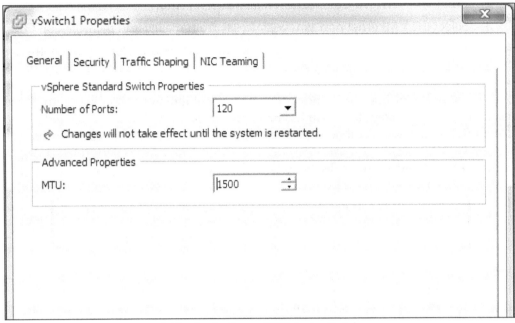

Setting Jumbo Frames MTU size in vSwitch

Although this is easy enough to change within vSphere itself by changing MTU on the vSwtich properties (see the preceding screenshot), the more challenging fact is that Jumbo Frames must be enabled on every single network device that the iSCSI packet traverses, as well as on the iSCSI array. If it isn't enabled on every device along its path, you will often see fragmented packets which ultimately lead to latency and disconnects from the storage device.

In order to confirm that we have Jumbo Frames set up properly in our environment, we can pass an MTU size to our vmkping command that we send to the storage array. The MTU size determined in vmkping is calculated by subtracting our header size from the MTU size we have set up on our vSwitch. In this case, using the standard Jumbo Frame MTU of 9000 and a header size of 28 bytes, we would use the following command to test our configuration:

```
vmkping -s 8972 -d 192.16.6.75
```

If we receive a response from the preceding command, it means that we are communicating with our storage array at the desired MTU size. If the command did not complete successfully, `vmkping` will return **sendto() failed (Message too long)** as a response. This indicates that we have some work to do somewhere down the line of network devices to allow Jumbo Frames to pass through.

Most of the best practices related to vSphere and iSCSI suggest implementing Jumbo Frames to gain more performance; however, we must ensure that in doing so, we have implemented the support for Jumbo Frames across the complete stack, from the host to the storage array.

Summary

Storage contention and performance issues are one of the most common causes of slowness and outages within vSphere. Due to the number of software and hardware components involved in the vSphere storage stack, it's hard for us to pinpoint exactly where the root cause of a storage contention issue is occurring. Using some of the tools, examples, features, and common causes explained in this chapter, we should be able to isolate issues, making it easier for us to troubleshoot and resolve problems.

We went through how to measure latency in a virtualized environment and how to properly calculate and size storage based on our IOPs requirements. We also explored some of the features that vSphere provides us with it help us better balance our workloads across datastores and maintain storage compliance as it relates to latency and performance. Additionally, we explored some of the common issues that affect storage contention and latency such as SCSI reservation conflicts and queue depth, as well as covering some common solutions to get more performance out of our NAS and iSCSI storage.

In the next chapter, we will explore issues affecting storage capacity management and over commitment.

5
Troubleshooting Storage Capacity and Overcommitment

So far, we covered how to deal with storage visibility, contention, and performance issues. This leaves us with the final vSphere topics which we will cover that can affect storage; capacity and overcommitment. This chapter will cover how to use some simple monitoring tools, alarms, and features included within vSphere that can help to alert us and resolve storage capacity problems. It is important to note that not all features are included in all licensing editions of vSphere, so we will also cover how to manually free up space on our datastores and how to extend or grow our datastores in the event that we no longer have free space available.

This chapter will cover the following:

- Monitoring datastore usage
- Thin Provisioning
- Snapshots
- Datastore file management
- Virtual machine swap files
- Increasing the size of our datastores
- Balancing capacity with Storage DRS

Monitoring datastore usage

When a VMFS datastore does not contain enough free space to efficiently operate, storage operations become fairly unpredictable and performance can suffer. We may experience things such as not being able to power on virtual machines, vMotion failures, poor or slow performance, and intermittent snapshot failures just to name a few. Needless to say, when we run out of space on a datastore, we will most certainly experience issues so we have to be sure that we always have free space available.

The question for us is how much free space do we need to have available? In KB article 1003412, VMware recommends that 200 MB of free capacity remaining be a threshold when we should take action. In practice, most vSphere and storage administrators would never let vSphere datastores get even close to the 200 MB threshold. The KB article 1003412 also states that a VMFS volume will only ever grow until there is 100 MB of free space. The 100 MB free space is a critical threshold which the system needs to maintain free in order to perform metadata updates. Again, most vSphere administrators are careful to ensure that vSphere Storage never reaches this threshold. Industry standards and best practices tend to recommend leaving around 15 to 20 percent of the total datastore space available.

> For more information in regards to troubleshooting datastore capacity, see KB article 1003412 located at `http://kb.vmware.com/selfservice/microsites/search.do?language=en_US&cmd=displayKC&externalId=1003412`.

Thankfully, vSphere displays datastore space consumption in many different places to help us avoid these situations; on the **Summary** tab of the host, on the **Storage** section of a host's **Configuration** tab, in the **Datastore and Datastore Clusters** inventory view, but my favorite shown in the following screenshot is the **Show All Datastores** storage view report:

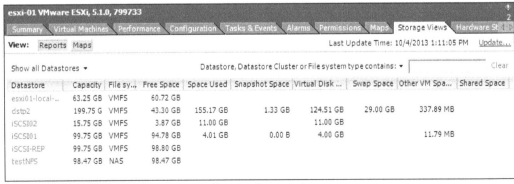

Storage view report

As illustrated in the preceding screenshot, this storage view allows us to dissect our datastore capacity into multiple sections such as the overall capacity, space used, free space, snapshot consumption, virtual disk consumption, and swap file usage. We can use these views to pinpoint the root cause when our datastores are nearing capacity, that is, we can decide whether to first investigate snapshots, virtual machine swap files, and so on.

As with most of the recommendations throughout this book, simply monitoring our storage through vSphere Client is not very effective. This is where vCenter alarms become important. vCenter contains a couple of default alarms relating to capacity; Datastore Cluster is out of space and Datastore usage on disk.

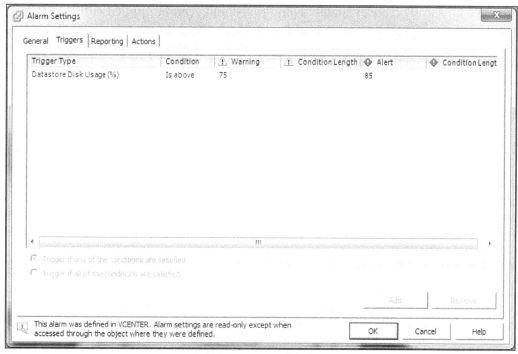

Datastore usage on disk alarm

Both the "Datastore cluster is out of space" and "Datastore Usage on Disk" alarms are defined on the vCenter object and are enabled by default. The preceding screenshot shows the **Datastore Disk Usage** alarm's warning level is set to **75** percent utilization and alert level is set to **85** percent.

> The default alarms for storage cannot be modified while on the **Datastores** view. We must be in **Hosts and Clusters** and on the vCenter instance in order to modify these alarms.

There are many factors that play a role in a datastore reaching capacity and running out of space. In the rest of this chapter, we will take a closer look at some of the most common scenarios that cause issues in terms of datastore capacity and how to resolve them.

Thin Provisioning

VMware vSphere allows us to maximize utilization of our storage by using a deployment method called Thin Provisioning. Thin-provisioned storage is presented in full to the guest VM, but the host and storage are only utilizing the actual data capacity that is in use. In turn, this allows us to provision more capacity to VMs than what we physically have available. Thin Provisioning can be applied either on the array level, the virtual disk level, or a mixture of both. In this chapter, we will focus mostly on virtual disk or hypervisor thin provisioning; however, both are explained in the following sections.

Array thin provisioning

Most storage arrays support array level thin provisioning on a LUN-by-LUN basis. When a thin-provisioned LUN is presented to a host, any thin or lazy zeroed virtual disks on that LUN will consume only the storage that they need, freeing up the space they would normally consume to be provisioned to other LUNs on the array. All the dynamic growing processes of a thinly-provisioned LUN on the array are handled by the array.

Hypervisor (VMDK) thin provisioning

This is essentially the same concept of array thin provisioning but instead applied to individual virtual disks. When we deploy a thin-provisioned disk at the hypervisor level to a LUN, only the capacity that the disk actually needs is consumed and the remaining space is still available for other virtual disks on that LUN. The utilized capacity, however, is abstracted from the guest OS, that is, the OS has no knowledge that it is thinly provisioned. The operating system will believe that it has all the storage that was allocated to it. When a write is issued to a virtual disk, the I/O is intercepted by vSphere and the virtual disk grows in small increments to handle the new data.

As mentioned before, Thin Provisioning allows us to better utilize our resources in terms of storage capacity. Say, for instance, we had an application that required 100 GB of free space to install and we knew, for a fact, that it was only ever going to use 20 GB. We could present the VM a thin-provisioned disk of 100 GB, allowing the application to be installed. In reality though, the disk consumption on the datastore will only be 20 GB, leaving 80 GB to be presented to other VMs.

The following screenshot illustrates the capacity section of a heavily over-provisioned datastore. As seen in the capacity table, we have roughly 200 GB of overall capacity. However, using Thin Provisioning, we have 487 GB of capacity provisioned to our VMs. By looking at the 42 GB of free space available, we can conclude that even though 487 GB has been provisioned, we are really only consuming around 160 GB.

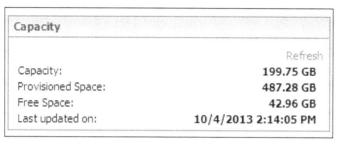

A heavily over-committed datastore.

As we can see, Thin Provisioning can be a valuable feature, and can save us costs on physical storage by using the overcommitment capabilities. One danger in this situation is the possibility that since we are over-allocating storage on our datastores, a few thin-provisioned VMs with sudden data growth could cause our datastore to fill up. In the event of the datastore reaching capacity, any thin-provisioned VM guests are at risk of halting. Thick-provisioned systems should continue to operate as they have already pre-allocated their storage. Thin-provisioned disk not only affect capacity but performance as well. This is particularly applicable to high I/O guests as the disk will take an extra I/O hit as it grows to capacity.

Monitoring Thin Provisioning

Given the preceding scenario, it is particularly important that we monitor any datastores which contain thin-provisioned disks. The easiest way to do this is through vCenter Server alarms. If we are using array-based thin provisioning and have a storage array that supports VAAI, an alarm (thin provision volume capacity threshold exceeded) will automatically be flagged when the consumption of the datastore reaches 75 percent. In terms of hypervisor thin provisioning, the "Datastore Disk Provisioned" alarm will alert us when we have exceeded a certain percentage relative to the overall capacity. This does not necessarily mean that action needs to be taken; it's just warning us of how over provisioned we are.

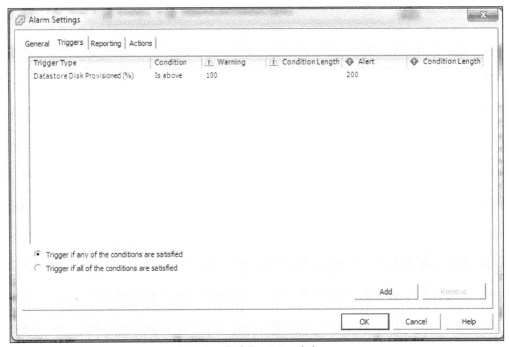

Datastore Disk Provisioned alarm

The following are the steps to setup the **Datastore Disk Provisioned** alarm.

1. From the **Alarms** tab, right-click on any whitespace and then select **New Alarm**.

2. Give the alarm a name, be sure **Datastore** is our **Monitor** object and select **Monitor for specific conditions or state, for example, CPU usage, power state**.

3. On the **Triggers** tab, click on **Add** to configure a new trigger. Select the **Datastore Disk Provisioned** trigger.

4. You can modify the default warning and alert thresholds. By default, they are set at **100** and **200** percent respectively which mean that if we over provision to the capacity of the datastore, a warning will be flagged. If we provision twice as much space as our datastore, then an alert will trigger.

5. On the **Actions** tab, we can set up any desired notifications we prefer.

> Although the risk of our datastores reaching capacity is evident, Thin Provisioning still gives the administrator many benefits in terms of cost savings. There are no best practices which state whether or not to use it. Knowing your workloads and VM change rates can be a key success factor in benefiting from Thin Provisioning.

Snapshots

Another valuable VMware vSphere feature is virtual machine snapshots. Snapshots give us the ability to capture **point in time** restore points on a virtual machine which can be utilized to test things such as upgrades, patch installations, and general configuration changes. If something were to go terribly wrong during our tests, snapshots give us the ability to failback or go to these points in time, the known good states.

Snapshots are often used in backup scenarios as well, where a snapshot will be taken to free up the underlying disk in order for it to be backed up or replicated. However, along with all of these benefits comes the drawback of the risk of a snapshot filling up a datastore if not closely monitored. To understand this, we will first look at what happens when a snapshot is taken.

Understanding vSphere Snapshots

A snapshot of a VM creates several new files on our datastore explained as follows:

* `.vmsd`: It contains information about the snapshot
* `.vmsm`: It contains a point in time copy of the VM's memory
* `.vmdk` and `delta.vmdk`: These are the pointer and virtual disk for each disk inside the VM

After the snapshot has created the .vmsd and .vmsm files, a thin-provisioned delta virtual disk is created for each virtual disk assigned to the VM. The original disk at this point will only process reads, and any changes to the VM will be forwarded to the delta disk. Although this delta disk is thin provisioned, it does have the ability to grow as large as the virtual disk it represents. The effects of the delta disk are illustrated in the following screenshot, where we can see that a VM that was initially 20 GB in size actually reports at 40 GB provisioned due to the delta files present:

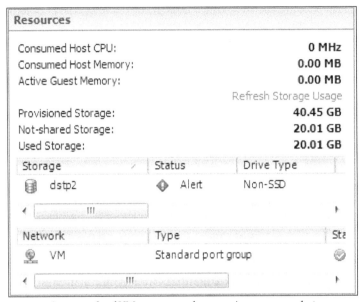

An example of VM resources when running on a snapshot

Additionally, vSphere supports up to 32 snapshots within any given snapshot chain. This is definitely not a best practice, but is something to pay particular attention to as your provisioned capacity can grow even larger. Snapshots can quickly pose a risk to our datastore capacity which is why it is very important that we utilize snapshots in a temporary manner and that we closely monitor their usage and growth to prevent unexpected datastore capacity issues.

Monitoring snapshot disk usage

vCenter provides us with an alarm that we can use to monitor the growth of snapshots and alert us when they grow to be a certain size. This alarm is called **VM Snapshot Size**.

VM Snapshot Size alarm.

The following are the steps to setup our **VM Snapshot Size** alarm:

1. From the **Alarms** tab, right-click on any whitespace and select **New Alarm**.

2. Give the alarm a name, be sure **Virtual Machines** is our **Monitor** object and select **Monitor for specific conditions or state, for example, CPU usage, power state**.

3. On the **Triggers** tab, click on **Add** to configure a new trigger. Select the **VM Snapshot Size (GB)** trigger.

4. This trigger has no default warning and alert thresholds. It may be good to begin by setting warning levels around 0.5 GB and alert levels at 1 GB, that is, if our snapshot grows to be at least 1 GB in size, an alert will be triggered.

5. On the **Actions** tab, we can set up any desired notifications we prefer.

As illustrated in the preceding screenshot, we can have vSphere alert us when a snapshot begins to grow larger than we might expect it to. vSphere also has a built-in alarm that will notify us if we have any snapshots requiring consolidation. This is a great alarm to have enabled due to the fact that this may be the only indicator available that a VM contains a snapshot.

At the very least, we should have the "Snapshot size" alarm set up to proactively alert us when snapshots are becoming too large. Large snapshots can take a very long time to commit or delete and depending on the size, for stability reasons, it may require that another small snapshot is taken before the consolidation can occur. Additionally, snapshots are easy to forget about as there is no indicator within vSphere Client, indicating whether the VM is running off or on. If a snapshot is left around for too long, we pose a big risk of filling up one of our datastores. It is also important to note that during snapshot deletion, additional disk space may be required depending on which vSphere version is in place. Prior to vSphere 4, during snapshot deletion, each snapshot would be merged into its parent in the snapshot tree before finally merging the last delta into the original disk. Only then would delta disks be deleted. Depending on the size and age of the snapshot, this could require us to have a significant amount of free space before we could consolidate. This is definitely not a good situation if we were already out of space.

Since vSphere 4.0, all deltas now consolidate back to the original virtual disk rather than into their parent snapshot. This process is performed sequentially and requires significantly less space. In fact, all that is required is capacity for one delta to accept any writes to the VM while consolidation is taking place. This is definitely more efficient and allows snapshot deletion to complete successfully in low space situations.

Despite VMware's best efforts to minimize the capacity requirement when deleting snapshots, there are times when we simply do not have enough free space to consolidate. Thankfully, there are a few solutions out there that address this. The first and by far the easiest is to Storage vMotion our VM to another datastore with available capacity. Since vSphere 5.0, Storage vMotion can migrate a VM containing snapshots. That said, if experiencing a snapshot deletion issue with an older version of vSphere, we can resort to cloning that VM to another datastore. During this operation, the VM must be powered off and the snapshots will not be preserved.

Datastore file management

Datastore file management is the simplest way to free up some space on our datastores. vSphere environments tend to be very dynamic in nature, with VMs being deployed and destroyed on multiple occasions. Often a VM will get created to perform a certain task or test and then abandoned. The VM will often be powered down and removed from inventory, leaving the files that make up that VM on the datastore.

Even though we have retired the application, powered down the VM, and removed it from inventory, the files that make up that VM still reside on the datastore and still consume space. And we aren't limited to just unregistered VMs in this case. A VMFS datastore can hold any type of file placed in it. Therefore, if we have placed ISO image files or other packages in our datastores, they will also contribute to the overall capacity usage.

So how do we find out what and where these files are? Unfortunately, there is no button that we can simply press to do this for us. There is, however, one feature of vSphere that we can use to help us, and that's Storage DRS maintenance mode. Earlier in the book, we discussed what Storage DRS can do for us in terms of contention, and later in this chapter, we will talk about how it can help us to balance our datastore capacity; however, in terms of file management, we will explore maintenance mode. Maintenance mode acts similar to that of putting a host in maintenance mode; however, instead of vMotioning VMs, it utilizes Storage vMotion to migrate VMs to other datastores within the cluster. While SDRS maintenance mode is designed for performing maintenance on the storage, it can be utilized to evacuate all registered VMs off the datastore. Any VMs or files that remain on a datastore in maintenance mode are unknown to vCenter and are usually safe to be deleted.

If we run into issues where a datastore has experienced an out-of-space condition, removing any of these foreign files and unregistered VMs will help us to claim back the space we may need to get our VMs un-paused, snapshots consolidated, and get back to running efficiently.

 Always ensure that any files you are removing from datastores are not needed. Although it goes against best practices, we have the ability to mount datastores to hosts belonging to different vCenter Server instances. This presents a challenge as we may conclude that the VM is not registered in one vCenter and process the deletion when the VM is actually registered to another vCenter server instance. Always take caution when performing direct deletions of a VM's files on a datastore.

Virtual machine swap files

Every time a virtual machine is powered on, a swap file (.vswp) is created. Swap files are utilized by ESXi to swap memory in and out of the disk in case of contention. Swap files affect capacity due to the fact that they are the same size of the memory allocated to that virtual machine, minus any reservations configured.

[

The .vswp files are unique to ESXi and used only for hypervisor functions, that is, they are different from those memory techniques that are applied from within the guest OS, such as the swap partition for Linux and the page file for Windows.
]

As we know, the configuration maximums continue to grow in each and every new release of ESXi, with the current version allowing a rather substantial 1 TB of memory to be assigned to a single virtual machine. If we have deployed this amount of RAM to a VM (with no memory reservation), then we would also end up with a 1 TB swap file on our datastores. This extra swap file consumption is often overlooked during capacity planning. As a more common example, let's say we had a VM with 8 GB of memory, powered off, on a datastore that had only 6 GB of free capacity. When we attempt to power on this VM, ESXi would return an error stating there is insufficient space on the datastore. This is because there is not enough space to create a .vswp file of 8 GB in size. So how would we get this VM to power on? Aside from using techniques explained in the chapter to free up space, there are a couple of things that we could do.

First, if we could modify the amount of assigned memory to the VM. Changing the VM's memory from 8 GB to 4 GB would result in the swap file requiring 4 GB of space rather than 8 GB, ultimately allowing our VM to be powered on. Second, we could change or add a memory reservation on the VM. Since reservations are guaranteed amounts of physical memory, they are not used in calculations by ESXi when creating swap files. Therefore, if we were to configure a reservation of 4 GB to our VM, our swap file consumption would be reduced to 4 GB in size (8 GB (allocated) - 4 GB (reserved)), ultimately allowing our VM to power on.

If we find ourselves out of space on a datastore, using some of the previously mentioned swap techniques could be a great way, especially if we have some VMs with larger amounts of memory, of freeing up space that ESXi needs in order to operate. Simply adding reservations to existing VMs, or powering off non-critical VMs that don't need to be running (since swap files are only present when VMs are powered on) could be a temporary solution that would free us up enough space to get our critical workloads running and give us enough time to fully address the capacity issue or extend some more free space on to the datastore.

Increasing the size of our datastores

Sometimes, no matter how many unwanted files or snapshots we remove, or how many swap files we manipulate, we simply cannot free up enough space on our datastores. At this point, the only option we have is to extend the VMFS datastore. vSphere has a couple of ways that can increase the size of our datastores. These include growing the existing datastore onto adjacent space or extending the datastore into additional LUNs. Although both techniques result in higher capacity, the processes and benefits differ and are explained in the next section.

Growing a VMFS datastore

As of vSphere 4.0, we have the ability to grow our VMFS volumes into adjacent free space in order to increase their capacity. In order to grow our volumes, we must first ensure that there is free space available on the LUN hosting the datastore. Typically, a vSphere administrator would format all available space on the LUN as a VMFS partition when it is presented to the ESXi host. This means that there is seldom space available that isn't part of the datastore. We can however, if our array supports it (most do), increase the size of our LUNs. This will add free space adjacent to our datastore allowing us to grow our VMFS volume and increase the capacity of the datastore.

The steps to grow a VMFS datastore are as follows:

1. Select the datastore you wish to grow from the **Storage** section of a host's **Configuration** tab, and then click on **Properties**.

2. Click on the **Increase** button and examine the list of storage devices available. If your volume is able to be expand into adjacent space, you will see that the **Expandable** column will be labeled **Yes**.

3. The disk layout window will show that we have one primary partition and the free space that we are expanding into. Click on **Next**.

4. In the **Extent Size** window, we can specify whether we would like to use all of the available free space or specify a custom amount to use. Most times we will just use all of it. Click on **Next**, and then click on **Finish**.

5. After storage rescan of our datastores, we should now see that the capacity reflects that of the free space we have added.

Adding an extent to a VMFS datastore

Adding an extent to an existing VMFS datastore is essentially spanning the VMFS file system across additional LUNs presented to the ESXi host. When we do this, the initial LUN, the one that we are attempting to extend becomes the **head extent**. Any additional LUNs that we extend to are considered **non-head** extents. By extending our datastore, we are taking the free space on additional LUNs and adding it to our initial datastore, ultimately increasing our capacity.

The steps to span a datastore onto an existing LUN are as follows:

1. Select the datastore you wish to add an extent to from the **Storage** section of a host's **Configuration** tab, and then click on **Properties**.

2. Click on the **Increase** button. From the list of storage devices, select which LUN you would like to add to the datastore as an extent, and then click on **Next**.

3. After examining the disk layout window, click on **Next**.

4. In the **Extent Size** window, we can specify whether we would like to use all of the available free space or specify a custom amount to use. Most times we will just use all of it. Click on **Next**, and then click on **Finish**.

5. After storage rescan of our datastores, we should now see that the capacity reflects that of the extents that we have added.

 When adding an extent, it is recommended to ensure that all LUNs included as extents have the same storage characteristics, disk types, and RAID levels. For example, we shouldn't span a LUN that has an underlying RAID 5 level onto a LUN that has RAID 1. We should also try and keep all extents on the same storage processor and storage array.

As stated before, both growing a VMFS volume and extending a VMFS volume will give us the same outcome, which is a higher capacity datastore.

Adding extents comes with its own challenges though. When we add extents to a datastore, we increase the complexity as well as the risks associated with that datastore. Although the datastore is still visible and accessible within vSphere, in the case we lose an extent (as long as it isn't the head extent), any VM I/O associated with the lost extent will ultimately fail and error. However, by adding extents we can reduce the need for SCSI reservations, since only the head extent will require that a SCSI reservation be issued. It is generally recommended to grow or expand our datastore into adjacent space if possible. When we grow our datastore, we are essentially mimicking the layout of a newly created datastore.

Balancing capacity with Storage DRS

We have discussed Storage DRS previously in *Chapter 4*, *Troubleshooting Storage Contention*, in terms of how it helps us balance I/O and performance, but it also helps us to balance our datastore capacity. In fact, Storage DRS can help us to prevent most if not all of the issues discussed in this chapter.

It does this by dynamically monitoring capacity and free space on all of the datastores contained within a datastore cluster. When the utilization hits a certain threshold (80 percent by default), SDRS will compute which VMs could be a candidate to move, and then leverage Storage vMotion to move the VMs and balance out the free space across all datastores within the cluster.

You can use the instructions in *Chapter 4*, *Troubleshooting Storage Contention*, to enable SDRS. One caveat is that SDRS is currently only available in Enterprise Plus licensing editions of vSphere. So if you have Enterprise Plus, I would definitely recommend enabling SDRS in your environment.

Summary

Storage capacity and overcommitment can cause us major issues and problems. This can easily be prevented by following some of the recommendations in this chapter. Keeping a close eye on our thin-provisioned disks and snapshots can go miles in ensuring that we always have enough capacity for vSphere to run efficiently. If we do encounter a capacity issue, apart from removing unwanted files, we can use the techniques to grow or extend our datastores to provide more capacity. Apart from setting up the alarms explained in this chapter, we can also prevent a storage capacity issue from occurring by leveraging Storage DRS inside our environments to proactively monitor the space utilization of our datastores and balance capacity as needed.

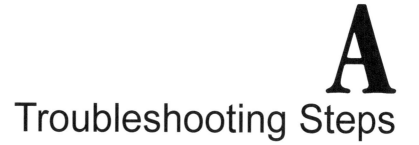

Troubleshooting Steps

You cannot connect to your iSCSI storage

The following are some questions and tasks that you can partake in to troubleshoot iSCSI connection failures.

Have all the network requirements for your iSCSI connection been met?

> You can refer *Chapter 3, Troubleshooting Storage Visibility,* for more information on this topic.

You need to consider the following points when checking network requirements:

- The ESXi host needs to have the proper networking configuration if using the software iSCSI initiator. A VMkernel port must be set up on the same subnet as your iSCSI storage array with the proper IP addressing and subnet mask.

- Ensure all DNS and routing information is accurate using the following command:

```
esxcfg-route -l
```

- If you are using VLANs, be sure that proper VLAN configuration has been implemented.

- Has the iSCSI storage array's IP address been entered in either the dynamic or static discovery tab?

- Is it possible to ping your storage array?

```
vmkping <IP OF ARRAY>
```

- Have all the proper ports (3260) been opened up for iSCSI communication? To test port connectivity from the ESXi host to your iSCSI storage array, use the following command:

```
nc -z <IP OF ARRAY> 3260
```

- Are there any firewalls in between your ESXi host and your iSCSI array? If so, ensure that the proper ports have been opened. To check the local firewall on ESXi, use the following command:

```
esxcli network firewall ruleset list | grep iSCSI
```

- Does your network utilize Jumbo Frames? If so, ensure Jumbo Frame configuration has been enabled on all devices the iSCSI packet will traverse. To ensure our vSwitch is configured with Jumbo Frames, use the following command:

```
esxcli network vswitch standard list
```

- To check that we properly have Jumbo Frames setup throughout the network stack, using the default 9000 MTU size, run the following command on an ESXi host:

```
vmkping -s 8972 -d <IP OF ARRAY>
```

Various things to check on ESXi

You can refer *Chapter 1, Understanding vSphere Storage Concepts and Methodologies,* and *Chapter 3, Troubleshooting Storage Visibility,* for more information on this topic.

The following items need to be checked on ESXi when troubleshooting iSCSI connection failures:

- Ensure that no claim rules have been added to the ESXi runtime utilizing the MASK_PATH plug-in. The following command will list your claim rules:

```
esxcli storage core claimrule list
```

- Ensure that LUN ID is set to a number below 255. Also, check the **Disk. MaxLun** advanced setting ensuring that your LUN ID isn't higher than the value configured.

Have all CHAP requirements been met?

 You can refer *Chapter 3, Troubleshooting Storage Visibility*, for more information on this topic.

The following items need to be checked for CHAP when troubleshooting iSCSI connection failures:

- Double check your CHAP settings
  - Ensure you have entered your CHAP user ID and secret properly in both the iSCSI array and ESXi
  - If using bidirectional CHAP, the CHAP secret must be different from the mutual CHAP secret

- Double check your target settings
  - By default when you enable CHAP, it is enabled on all iSCSI targets since it is inherited. If using CHAP on some targets and not others, be sure to check your CHAP settings on individual targets and if not required, override the **Inherit from parent** option.

- See *Further check the logs for iSCSI-related errors* and *Appendix C, iSCSI Error Codes*, to determine if there are any further CHAP related errors occurring

Has there been any advanced settings dealing with iSCSI incorrectly configured?

There are a variety of advanced settings that may affect your connection to your iSCSI storage array:

- **LoginTimeout**: By default, it is set to 5 seconds. It specifies that time in seconds that an initiator will wait for login response. If this is set to low or we are experiencing contention, we may need to increase this parameter. The recommended value is 5.

- **RecoveryTimeout**: By default, it is set to 10 seconds. It specifies the time in seconds that can elapse while a session recovery is performed. If the recovery hasn't completed within this time, the initiator will terminate the session. If this value is set too low, we could be experiencing path thrashing. If set too high, we could be waiting too long to fail a path. The recommended Value is 10.

- **Header and Data Digests**: It is set to **Prohibited** by default. It can be enabled to ensure data integrity. For troubleshooting, it is recommended to be to **Prohibited**. The recommended value is **Prohibited**.

Further check the logs for iSCSI-related errors

 You can refer *Chapter 3, Troubleshooting Storage Visibility*, for more information on this topic.

The following items need to be considered when checking logs for troubleshooting iSCSI connection failures:

- We can further view any iSCSI-related errors in the logs by filtering the entire log folder with the following command:

```
grep -r iscsid /var/log/* | less
```

- Refer *Appendix C, iSCSI Error Codes*, to interpret any reason codes returned

- Verbose logging can be enabled for troubleshooting purposes by running the following command:

```
vmkiscsid -x "insert into internal (key,value) VALUES
  ('option.LogLevel','999');"
```

You cannot connect to your NFS storage

The following are some questions and tasks you can take to troubleshoot NFS connection issues.

Have all the network requirements for you NFS connection been met?

[🔅 You can refer *Chapter 3, Troubleshooting Storage Visibility*, for more information on this topic.]

You need to consider the following points when checking network requirements:

- The ESXi host needs to have the proper networking configuration in order to attach to an NFS mount. A VMkernel port must be set up on the same subnet as your NFS storage array with the proper IP addressing and subnet mask.

- Ensure all DNS and routing information is accurate using the following command:

  ```
  esxcfg-route -l
  ```

- If you are using VLANs, be sure that proper VLAN configuration has been implemented.

- Is it possible to ping your storage array?

  ```
  vmkping <IP OF ARRAY>
  ```

- Have all the proper ports (2049/111) been opened up for NFS communication. To test port connectivity from the ESXi host to your NFS storage array, use the following command:

  ```
  nc -z <IP OF ARRAY> 2049
  ```

- Are there any firewalls in between your ESXi host and your NFS array? If so, ensure that the proper ports have been opened. To check the local firewall on ESXi, use the following command:

  ```
  esxcli network firewall ruleset list | grep nfsClient
  ```

- Does your network utilize Jumbo Frames? If so, ensure Jumbo Frame configuration has been enabled on all devices the NFS packet will traverse. To check that we properly have Jumbo Frames set up, using the default 9000 MTU size, run the following command on an ESXi host:

  ```
  vmkping -s 8972 -d <IP OF ARRAY>
  ```

Check the settings on your NFS array

[🔆 You can refer *Chapter 3, Troubleshooting Storage Visibility*, for more information on this topic.]

You need to consider the following points when checking settings on your NFS array:

- Have all of your ESXi hosts been added properly in the NFS ACL list on your storage array?
- Have the proper permissions been applied to your NFS exports. ESXi, at the very least, will need read/write permissions in order to write to the datastore.
- ESXi supports only NFS Version 3. Be sure your NFS storage array also supports NFS Version 3.

Has there been any advanced settings dealing with NFS incorrectly configured?

There are a variety of advanced settings that may affect your connection to your NFS storage array:

- **NFS.MaxVolumes**: By default, it is set to 8. This represents the maximum number of NFS volumes that an ESXi host can mount. You may need to change this number if this is the ninth volume on the host. This must match on all hosts. If changing, this recommendation is normally to change the TCP/IP heap settings as well. The recommended value is **Varies**.
- **Net.TcpIpHeapSize** and **Net.TcpIpHeapMax**: By default, size is 0 and max is 64 MB. These represent the size and maximum memory that is allocated to TCP/IP. Storage vendors normally make recommendations as to what this value should be. The recommended value is **Varies**.
- **NFS.DiskFileLockUpdateFreq**: By default, it is set to 10 seconds. It represents the time between updates to a disk lock file. Too high of a value will increase the time it takes to recover from stale locks. Be sure that all hosts contain the same value. The recommended value is 10

Further check the logs for NFS related errors

 You can refer *Chapter 3, Troubleshooting Storage Visibility,* for more information on this topic.

The following items need to be considered when checking logs for NFS storage:

- We can further view any NFS related errors in the logs by grepping the entire log folder with the following command:

```
grep -r nfs /var/log/* | less
```

- Verbose logging can be enabled for troubleshooting purposes by running the following command:

```
esxcfg-advcfg -s 1 /NFS/LogNfsStat3
```

You cannot connect to your Fibre Channel Storage

The following are some questions and tasks you can take to troubleshoot Fibre Channel connection issues.

Fibre Channel switch zoning

[💡 You can refer *Chapter 3, Troubleshooting Storage Visibility,* for more information on this topic.]

Ensure that your WWNs on your HBAs have been correctly zoned to see the Fibre Channel storage array.

Check paths to storage array/PSP

[You can refer *Chapter 1, Understanding vSphere Storage Concepts and Methodologies*, for more information on this topic.]

The following items need to be considered when checking path to storage array:

- Ensure that the correct Path Selection Policy has been selected for the type of storage array that you are using:
    - ○ VMW_PSP_FIXED: Default for active-active arrays
    - ○ VMW_PSP_MRU: Default for active-passive arrays

- To list your currently loaded PSP, use the following command:

```
esxcli storage nmp device list
```

Various things to check on ESXi

[You can refer *Chapter 3, Troubleshooting Storage Visibility*, for more information on this topic.]

The following items need to be checked on ESXi:

- Ensure that no claim rules have been added to the ESXi runtime utilizing the MASK_PATH plug-in. The following command will list your claim rules:

```
esxcli storage core claimrule list
```

- Ensure that LUN ID is set to a number below 255. Also, check the **Disk. MaxLun** advanced setting ensuring that your LUN ID isn't higher than the value configured.

Check the storage array

Some storage arrays will implement soft zoning and ways to mask LUNs from hosts. Check your storage array to ensure that the LUNs are all presented to the ESXi hosts.

Further check the logs for Fibre Channel related errors

[💡 You can refer *Chapter 3, Troubleshooting Storage Visibility*, for more information on this topic.]

The following items need to be considered when checking logs for Fibre Channel related errors:

- We can further view any Fibre Channel related errors in the logs by grepping the entire log folder with the following command. You may need to filter out any entries relating to iSCSI.

  ```
  grep -r SCSI /var/log/*  | less
  ```

- Verbose logging can be enabled for troubleshooting purposes by setting the bit values on the following advance settings.
  - **Scsi.LogCmdErrors**
  - **Scsi.LogScsiAborts**

My storage/virtual machine is slow

The following are some questions and tasks you can take to troubleshoot slow or poor storage performance.

Inspect latency values to further pinpoint where performance degradation is occurring

[💡 You can refer *Chapter 4, Troubleshooting Storage Contention*, for more information on this topic.]

Using esxtop and thresholds in *Appendix B, Statistics of esxtop*, inspect latency statistics (DAVG, KAVG, QAVG, and GAVG).

- High DAVG indicates a performance issue on the storage array or somewhere along the path to it.
- High KAVG indicates a performance issue within the VMkernel. Possible causes could include queuing, drivers, and so on.

- High QAVG indicates a performance issue is causing queue latency to go up. This could be an indicator of underperforming storage if higher DAVG numbers are experienced as well.

- High GAVG is normally the total of the three previous counters. If experiencing high GAVG while other latency metrics seem sufficient, the issue could reside within the VM drivers or virtual hardware.

Ensure that your storage array is handling the demand

 You can refer *Chapter 4, Troubleshooting Storage Contention,* and *Chapter 5, Troubleshooting Storage Capacity and Overcommitment,* for more information on this topic.

The following items need to be considered when dealing with storage arrays:

- Using the formulas from *Chapter 4, Troubleshooting Storage Contention,* calculate on a per-LUN basis your functional IOPs requirements

- Using esxtop and thresholds in *Appendix B, Statistics of esxtop,* inspect both ABORT and QUEUE statistics

  ○ Queuing and frequent command aborts could be a possible indicator of underperforming storage

- Check to see if the VM has a storage profile attached to it that may have gone out of compliance

- If possible, migrate your workload to a faster performing disk set or to a LUN with a different RAID type

- Using esxtop and thresholds in *Appendix B, Statistics of esxtop,* check to see if the issue is being caused by SCSI reservation conflicts or queue depth

  ○ For SCSI reservation conflicts, monitor CONS/s

  ○ For queue depth issues, monitor QUED

- If possible, enable Storage DRS to automatically balance your workloads

B

Statistics of esxtop

Overview of esxtop's interactive commands

There are many different interactive commands that can be run while executing **esxtop** to help you troubleshoot and identify issues. We can use the following guide to aide us in our esxtop usage.

Activating different displays

esxtop provides us with eight different displays that we can switch to in order to troubleshoot different ESXi components by pressing their corresponding character.

Component	Character	Description
CPU	c	Displays information regarding CPU resource usage
Interrupt	i	Displays information regarding CPU interrupt on VMkernel devices
Memory	m	Displays information regarding memory resource usage
Power management	p	Displays information regarding power usage per CPU
Network	n	Displays information regarding network resource usage
Disk device	u	Displays information regarding usage of disk devices (LUNs/Datastores)

Component	Character	Description
Disk adapter	d	Displays information regarding your disk adapters in the host (HBAs)
Disk VM	v	Displays information regarding the usage of your virtual disks inside the VMs

Field selection

There are many fields available for each view which are not shown by default. To add or remove fields from the display press the *F* key.

When the field list selection appears, press the corresponding character of the field to toggle whether it is displayed or not.

Field order

Each esxtop display screen has a default order that applies to the statistics it displays. This order can be changed by pressing the *O* key.

When the field list order screen appears, press the corresponding character of the field to move the field either right or left in the order sequence. Use the uppercase version of a character to move the field left and the lowercase version to move the field right.

Filtering and sorting the displayed objects

We are able to filter the objects (worlds) that esxtop displays in many different ways.

- To filter or limit display by a single group, press *L*, type the corresponding world/group ID and hit *Enter*. To remove filter press *L* and *Enter*.

- To view only instances related to VMs, press *V*. Pressing *V* again will restore all worlds.

- To view only a certain number of results press #, enter the desired number and press *Enter*. Using 0 as the desired number will display all results.

- On certain views you are able to expand or rollup statistics as they are shown as aggregated data by default. To do so, press *E* and enter the desired data to expand/rollup.

- To sort by certain columns, press *H* to enter the help screen. Under the **Sort by:** section, make a note of the desired column to sort by. Press any key to return to the main statistics screen and press the desired character of the column to sort.

Other useful information

The following bullet points outline some other useful commands and switches that esxtop contains:

- To change the default refresh level, press *S* and enter the desired refresh interval in seconds.

- To save your current configuration of column orders, sort fields, and so on, press *W* and enter a filename.

- To load esxtop and apply a configuration file, start esxtop with the `-c <configfile>` option.

- esxtop can also be run in batch mode which will capture results to a CSV file. This is done by specifying `-b` when starting esxtop and output to a filename.

- There are many different command line options you can also pass when running esxtop in batch mode. For a complete list, run `esxtop -h`.

 VMware has an application available for download that allows you to view esxtop from within a GUI interface called Visual esxtop. For more information, visit `http://labs.vmware.com/flings/visualesxtop`.

esxtop statistics

esxtop collects an abundance of statistics regarding all aspects of how your ESXi host and VMs are performing. Although it is possible to view metrics in regards to CPU, memory, and networking as well, I've only outlined the storage-related metrics here. The thresholds listed here are simply suggested values, thresholds that I've seen used in many whitepapers, VMware documentation, and resources in the past. There are many different reasons why a threshold could be met, so these are certainly not hard numbers.

Have a look at the following table:

Statistic	Description	Threshold
CMDS/s	Number of commands issued per second.	varies
READS/s	Number of read commands issued per second.	varies
WRITES/s	Number of write commands issued per second.	varies
MBREAD/s	Megabytes read per second.	varies
MBWRTN/s	Megabytes written per second.	varies

Statistic	Description	Threshold
DAVG/cmd	Latency observed by the device driver—roundtrip latency from HBA to storage array. Sustained thresholds usually indicate a performance issue with the underlying storage.	25
KAVG/cmd	Latency observed inside the VMkernel. Value should always be very low if not 0 unless queuing is observed.	1
QAVG/cmd	Latency observed inside the queue. This is part of KAVG/cmd. Sustained values indicate an issue with queuing or queue depth.	1
GAVG/cmd	Round trip latency as observed by the guest OS. Normally a total of DAVG, KAVG, and QAVG.	25
AQLEN	The storage adapter queue length—maximum number of active commands the adapter is configured for.	n/a
LQLEN	The LUN queue depth—maximum number of active commands the LUN can have.	n/a
WQLEN	The world queue depth—maximum number of active commands the world can contain.	n/a
ACTV	The number of commands that are currently active within the VMkernel.	varies
QUED	The number of commands that are currently queued in the VMkernel waiting for processing. Sustained thresholds may indicate a need to increase queue depth or an issue with the underlying storage array.	1
%USD	The percentage of queue depth used by active commands. Normally sits close to 0 unless queuing is occurring.	1
LOAD	The total number of active and queued commands as compared to queue depth. Should always be 0 unless queuing is occurring.	1
ABRTS/s	The number of commands that have been aborted per second. Normally indicates that the underlying storage is unable to meet the demands of your workloads.	1
RESETS/s	The number of commands reset per second.	1
RESV/s	The number of SCSI reservations issued per second.	n/a
CONS/s	The number of SCSI reservations conflicts occurring per second. Sustained high values could indicate that actions need to be taken to balance the metadata heavy operations.	20

C
iSCSI Error Codes

Interpreting software iSCSI error codes

The following table provides us with the information we need to decipher a software iSCSI error code in the vSphere logfiles. If the code is displayed as decimal, we can simply use the decimal column. If the code is displayed as an 8-digit hex code, in order to read it properly, we need to split it into two 4-digit hex numbers and use the Hex Code column. For example, I.E. 00050201 becomes 0005 and 0201.

Hex Code	Decimal Code	Source	Description
0000	0	Initiator	No Error
0001	1	Initiator	Generic Error
0002	2	Initiator	Object Not Found
0003	3	Initiator	Out of Memory
0004	4	Initiator	Transport Failure: This is a common error and indicates a network problem preventing the initiator from reaching the target
0005	5	Initiator	Login Failure: Check for a target-related code to determine if the login failed due to something on the array side
0006	6	Initiator	Database Failure
0007	7	Initiator	Invalid Operation
0008	8	Initiator	Transport Timeout: Cannot connect to the target before the timeout value expired and occurs due to array or network congestion
0009	9	Initiator	Internal Initiator Engine Fault
000a	10	Initiator	Logout Failure

Hex Code	Decimal Code	Source	Description
000b	11	Initiator	PDU send/receive timeout: Initiator established a socket/link to the target and sent the Login Request PDU, but has not received an answer from the target within the specified time and the Initiator aborted the login
000c	12	Initiator	Transport not found
000d	13	Initiator	Access error
000e	14	Initiator	Transport capabilities error: This should never be seen in a production environment with any supported iSCSI HBA/Driver
000f	15	Initiator	Object exists
0010	16	Initiator	Invalid request
0011	17	Initiator	iSNS server is unavailable
0012	18	Initiator	`vmkiscsid` daemon communications error
0000	NA	Target	No Error
0101	NA	Target	Target temporarily moved: The requested target has moved to a new IP address, but the change is not permanent
0102	NA	Target	Target permanently moved: The requested target has moved to a new IP address and the change is permanent
0200	NA	Target	Miscellaneous initiator failure
0201	NA	Target	Authentication failure
0202	NA	Target	Authorization failure: The initiator is denied access to attempt to login
0203	NA	Target	Not Found: The requested target does not exist at this address
0204	NA	Target	Target removed
0205	NA	Target	Unsupported version
0206	NA	Target	Too many connections: The array can no longer service incoming sessions as it is at capacity
0207	NA	Target	Missing parameter
0208	NA	Target	Cannot include in session
0209	NA	Target	Session type not supported
020a	NA	Target	Requested session does not exist
020b	NA	Target	Invalid request type during login

Hex Code	Decimal Code	Source	Description
0300	NA	Target	Target error (hardware or software)
0301	NA	Target	Service unavailable
0302	NA	Target	Out of resources

 For more information on iSCSI software initiator error codes, read the VMware KB Article 2012171 located at `http://kb.vmware.com/selfservice/microsites/search.do?language=en_US&cmd=displayKC&externalId=2012171`.

Index

Registered State Change Notification. *See* RSCN
Remote Procedure Call (RPC) 9
REPORT LUNS 10
reports view 24, 25
resxtop. *See* also esxtop 27
Round Robin path policy 89-91
RSCN 50
runtime names 15

S

Same Host and Transports Filter 44
SCSI reservation conflicts
  about 77, 78
  monitoring, with esxtop 79
  resolving 80-83
SDRS
  about 72, 75-77
  datastore capacity, balancing with 109
security models, vSphere 56
SIOC 77
software iSCSI error codes
  interpreting 125, 126
  URL 127
soft zoning. *See* WWN zoning
Storage Array Type Plugin (SATP)
  about 41
  commands 17
  roles 17
storage connections 10
storage contention
  disk adapter latency statistics 63, 64
  disk device latency statistics 64, 65
  identifying 62, 63
  latency monitoring, vCenter alarms
    used 66, 67
  virtual machine latency statistics 65, 66
Storage DRS. *See* SDRS
Storage I/O Control. *See* SIOC
storage performance issues
  identifying 62, 63
storage queues
  about 83
  adapter queue 84
  OS queue 83

per-LUN queue 84
viewing, in ESXi 84-86
storage, sizing
  disk requirements, calculating 69, 70
  IOPs, monitoring 71
  IOPs requisites, calculating 68
Storage Views tab
  about 23
  maps section 26
storage virtualization 8
swap files 106

T

T10 identifiers 14
thin provisioning
  about 98
  array thin provisioning 98
  hypervisor thin provisioning 98, 99
  monitoring 100, 101
top-level troubleshooting flow 23
troubleshooting Fibre Channel connection
    issues
  ESXi, checking 118
  Fibre Channel switch zoning 117
  logs, checking 119
  path, checking 118
  storage array, checking 118
troubleshooting, Fibre Channel storage
    visibility 49, 50
troubleshooting, IP storage visibility 51
troubleshooting iSCSI connection failures
  advanced settings, checking 113, 114
  CHAP requirements, checking 113
  ESXi, checking 112
  logs, checking 114
  network requirements, checking 111, 112
troubleshooting, iSCSI storage
    performance 89
troubleshooting NFS connection issues
  advanced settings, checking 116
  logs, checking 117
  network requirements, checking 115
  NFS array settings, checking 116
troubleshooting slow storage performance
  latency values, inspecting 119
  storage array, dealing with 120

LUN masking 38-41
LUN, numbering 48, 49
PSP 41-44
vCenter Server Storage filters 44-46
**vStorage APIs for Array
Integration (VAAI) 78**

W

World Wide Name (WWN) 50
WWN zoning 50

Thank you for buying
Troubleshooting vSphere Storage

About Packt Publishing

Packt, pronounced 'packed', published its first book "Mastering phpMyAdmin for Effective MySQL Management" in April 2004 and subsequently continued to specialize in publishing highly focused books on specific technologies and solutions.

Our books and publications share the experiences of your fellow IT professionals in adapting and customizing today's systems, applications, and frameworks. Our solution based books give you the knowledge and power to customize the software and technologies you're using to get the job done. Packt books are more specific and less general than the IT books you have seen in the past. Our unique business model allows us to bring you more focused information, giving you more of what you need to know, and less of what you don't.

Packt is a modern, yet unique publishing company, which focuses on producing quality, cutting-edge books for communities of developers, administrators, and newbies alike. For more information, please visit our website: www.packtpub.com.

About Packt Enterprise

In 2010, Packt launched two new brands, Packt Enterprise and Packt Open Source, in order to continue its focus on specialization. This book is part of the Packt Enterprise brand, home to books published on enterprise software – software created by major vendors, including (but not limited to) IBM, Microsoft and Oracle, often for use in other corporations. Its titles will offer information relevant to a range of users of this software, including administrators, developers, architects, and end users.

Writing for Packt

We welcome all inquiries from people who are interested in authoring. Book proposals should be sent to author@packtpub.com. If your book idea is still at an early stage and you would like to discuss it first before writing a formal book proposal, contact us; one of our commissioning editors will get in touch with you.

We're not just looking for published authors; if you have strong technical skills but no writing experience, our experienced editors can help you develop a writing career, or simply get some additional reward for your expertise.

vSphere High Performance Cookbook

ISBN: 978-1-78217-000-6   Paperback: 240 pages

Over 60 recipes to help you improve vSphere performance and solve problems before they arise

1. Troubleshoot real-world vSphere performance issues and identify their root causes

2. Design and configure CPU, memory, networking, and storage for better and more reliable performance

3. Comprehensive coverage of performance issues and solutions including vCenter Server design and virtual machine and application tuning

VMware vSphere 5.1 Cookbook

ISBN: 978-1-84968-402-6   Paperback: 466 pages

Over 130 task-oriented recipes to install, configure, and manage various vSphere 5.1 components

1. Install and configure vSphere 5.1 core components

2. Learn important aspects of vSphere such as administration, security, and performance

3. Configure vSphere Management Assistant(VMA) to run commands/scripts without the need to authenticate every attempt

Please check **www.PacktPub.com** for information on our titles

VMware Workstation - No Experience Necessary

ISBN: 978-1-84968-918-2   Paperback: 136 pages

Get started with VMware Workstation to create virtual machines and a virtual testing platform

1. Create virtual machines on Linux and Windows hosts

2. Create advanced test labs that help in getting back to any Virtual Machine state in an easy way

3. Share virtual machines with others, no matter which virtualization solution they're using

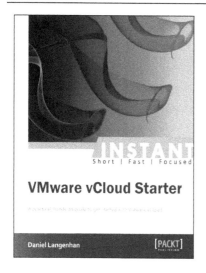

Instant VMware vCloud Starter

ISBN: 978-1-84968-996-0   Paperback: 76 pages

A practical, hands-on guide to get started with VMware vCloud

1. Learn something new in an Instant! A short, fast, focused guide delivering immediate results

2. Deploy and operate a VMware vCloud in your own demo kit

3. Understand the basics about the cloud in general and why there is such a hype

4. Build and use templates to quickly deploy complete environments

Please check **www.PacktPub.com** for information on our titles

www.ingramcontent.com/pod-product-compliance
Lightning Source LLC
Chambersburg PA
CBHW060147060326
40690CB00018B/4014